A Guide in Colour to
KITCHEN HERBS
AND SPICES

A Guide in Colour to

KITCHEN HERBS AND SPICES

By Bohumír Hlava and Dagmar Lánská
Edited by Morag Neil

TREASURE PRESS

Text by B. Hlava and D. Lánská

Illustrations: K. Hísek, J. Kaplická, J. Krejča, Z. Krejčová, F. Severa, B. Vančura, L. Wagner

Translated by Dana Hábová

First published in Great Britain in 1980 by
Octopus Books Limited

This edition published in 1990 by
Treasure Press
Michelin House
81 Fulham Road
London SW3 6RB

ISBN 1 85051 462 3

Printed in Czechoslovakia

3/99/33/51-02

Contents

What are Herbs and Spices?

Human life has always been closely related to the availability of useful plants — people have been dependent on plants since history began and no doubt will continue to be so. The versatility of many plants has been exploited to meet man's various needs; plants provide not only food, clothing, and building materials, but also important medicaments and many aromatic substances.

Everything we eat (except medicaments and chemicals) may be defined as comestibles, which can be divided into two groups: firstly, foodstuffs (such as flour, meat, potatoes and milk) which have specific food values and supply energy and essential materials to maintain the body's structure; secondly, aromatic substances, such as tea, coffee, cocoa and other plant products used as seasonings for food. These substances, mainly of vegetable origin, mostly lack any real food value but are endowed with other qualities such as a distinct flavour and aroma, and have a therapeutic effect on the digestive or nervous system. Known as herbs and spices, these substances are used in moderate quantities in the preparation of meals and drinks, to enhance flavour, add aromatic odour, and, in the case of spices, to add pungency or piquancy too. Herbs may be defined as the leaves or stalks of plants, either fresh, dried or otherwise prepared, whereas spices are usually thought of as coming from the seeds, berries or bark of a plant.

Neither herbs nor spices can be used in very large quantities in cooking without unpleasant effects. They will either make the dish too strong or possibly too bitter, and in very large quantities they can be harmful to the body.

A whole culture has grown up around herbs and spices and they have been purported through the ages to have many magical qualities. The popularity of spices grew to such an extent that the spice trade, for example, was one of the most lucrative trades of all. In the days when meat and fish had to be stored without the benefit of refrigeration, spice was a very necessary ingredient in cooking to make the food palatable. It is therefore not surprising that it was very highly valued, nor that its origins are mainly in the Far East where the climate is hotter and food deteriorates faster. Spicy food is, in fact, still more popular in the Far East than it is in Europe.

The actual properties of some herbs and spices play an important part in their use in cooking, as they can work to help the digestion, or act as an antiseptic, for example.

Any good cook will keep a range of spices in her kitchen, and grow some of the basic herbs in her garden, as most herbs are more pungent fresh than dried. In the case of both herbs and spices, the characteristic strong taste and aroma of the plants are caused by the presence of essential or volatile oils. In addition to these oils, herbs and spices may contain alkaloids, glycosides, pigments, phytoncides and other ingredients.

Today food stores and supermarkets stock a vast array of dried or ground herbs and mixed spices, often of synthetic origin or cultivated using quantities of chemicals such as fertilizers and pesticides. As we should not add more chemicals to our food than we absolutely have to, it is better to use natural herbs and spices whenever possible. Many of these are not difficult to grow, even if you have no garden.

As well as being an indispensable component of the diet from an aesthetic point of view, in supplying an attractive fragrance, taste and aroma, herbs also promote digestion and have preserving and even healing effects. Indeed, all the well-known herbs and spices were in fact once used medicinally and were sometimes considered to wield a miraculous power. Today they are still used to treat certain ailments, particularly in folk medicine.

The recommendations in this book are only of a generally informative character, and the doctor's advice should always be followed.

The Origin and Geographical Distribution of Spices

The most important spices originated in the tropics: Asia, Africa and South America. Spices were once a very valuable commodity and as a result the spice trade was much fought over.

Spice was easily stored and its price in relation to its weight was extremely high: for this reason it became an ideal merchandise for the trans-oceanic trade, particularly at a time when transport was limited and primitive.

In the Middle Ages, Arabian, Indian and Malaysian ships brought exotic spices into Arabian harbours, from where they were taken by caravan to ports in the eastern Mediterranean and thence to Europe. Venetian and Muslim merchants dominated this trade for a long time.

The desire to discover the shortest route to the Indies and thus reduce the price of spice was probably one of the reasons for Columbus's voyages to the west. Though he rediscovered America, he regretted, till the day he died, that he had not found a new passage to India.

Gradually, European powers became involved in the spice trade, attracted by the possibility of making huge profits. The Portuguese were one of the first European powers to participate in the spice trade. They made several reconnaissance voyages but the decisive one was the expedition of Vasco da Gama in 1497–1498. He succeeded in sailing around Africa, thus discovering a new route to India. In spite of intrigues and the fierce resistance of the Muslim traders, the Portuguese managed to establish direct commercial contact and their ships returned laden with spice. Spice trading consequently moved from Venice to Lisbon.

The Spanish followed on but were soon overtaken by the more successful Dutch. Their spice expeditions at the end of the 16th century pushed the Portuguese completely out of the world spice market and they carefully guarded their monopoly.

Colonial control of the spice trade hindered the wider distribution of the main spices. In Ceylon, for example, the Dutch safeguarded the growing of cinnamon by a law which punished trespass with the death penalty. Similarly, cultivation of clove and nutmeg was protected by Dutch law.

For a long time, Amsterdam was the capital of the spice trade, but in 1616, when the British consolidated their rule in India, the spice trade became their monopoly, and the Dutch were driven out.

Nevertheless, despite all obstructions and laws, the cultivation of rare spices extended into other, climatically similar areas. It is interesting that the country or area of origin of some spice species does not necessarily have to be the most important producer or exporter. In 1770, for instance, the French succeeded in introducing cloves to the islands of Mauritius and Réunion, from which the species was soon distributed, mainly to Zanzibar. The world stores of cloves soon rose, even though the homeland of the clove, the Moluccas, was no longer the major producer.

There are also numerous species of aromatic plants in the temperate zone. The evergreen 'maquis' in the Mediterranean is the source of many species, including savory, thyme, hyssop, lavender, mint, balm, rosemary, sage and many others. Some spices from the carrot family, such as cumin, parsley, coriander and fennel, also originate from these areas; they were introduced to central Europe in the early Middle Ages (9th to 12th centuries).

The universally used marjoram has its origin in North Africa and India. Sweet or red peppers apparently came to Europe in two ways: firstly from Mexico with Columbus's expedition to the Americas; and secondly from Asia to Hungary via Turkey. The original habitat of saffron was western Asia, from where it was distributed to India, China and then to Europe — to Spain and France.

Nowadays, these plants are cultivated all over the world. The young fresh leaves of coriander are used to season meat in Armenia and Georgia where it is called *kindze*. South Americans season their meat in the same way and call coriander *cilantro*. Spices of the temperate zone are cultivated in tropical and sub-tropical regions. Thanks to a well-developed trade, many spices are used all over the world.

Herbs and Spices Throughout History

Spices were probably first used in the Middle Stone Age, as seasonings to improve the flavour of meat, although it is possible that prehistoric man had already used leaves, roots, tubers, rhizomes and fruits found in nature as spices. The findings from the New Stone Age show that cumin may be the very oldest spice, but finds of poppy and angelica also date from this period.

Many plants, used at present as condiments, were in the past exploited as medicaments. The effects of exotic spices were often exaggerated and even sometimes regarded as miraculous. The first written documents on spice are from Mesopotamia and date from the 2nd and 3rd millennia BC. They mention, for example, *Asa foetida* (giant fennel), cassia, onion, garlic, fennel, saffron, thyme, mustard, cumin, dill, coriander, portulaca, liquorice, juniper, olives, pomegranates and bay leaf, all used as medicaments and seasonings. The Babylonians were not only successful cultivators of spice but also good traders. Likewise, the Persians grew numerous onion and garlic species; saffron and coriander were their favourite seasonings and they also used rose-water.

Some of the spices recommended and described in this book act as aphrodisiacs: for example, sesame, saffron, garlic, pepper, ginger, nutmeg and white mustard. Europe can be grateful to India for cumin, pepper, ginger, cardamom, cloves, lesser galangel, turmeric, nutmeg and mace. Certain spices in India were used as antitoxins (various peppers and ginger) or in everyday hygiene, for example, pepper mixed with ginger was used for cleaning teeth.

China has preserved many more written documents on spice than India. From the period between 2200–1080 BC there were reports by the emperors Cheng-nung and Chung-ti, founders of agriculture and medicine. The Chinese used star anise, pomegranate, saffron; they knew of celery, ginger, cumin, flag, tarragon, liquorice, nutmeg and mugwort.

The favourite seasonings and medicaments in Ancient Egypt were onion, garlic, juniper, coriander, cumin, parsley, celery, pomegranate and olives. These were being used some 3000 years ago. In a later period, as we know from a papyrus scroll dated 1500 BC, the list was complemented by mugwort, flag, anise, mustard, mint, saffron, cinnamon, sesame and many other culinary and medicinal plants. Many plants were used not only for healing or culinary purposes but also in cosmetics.

Central and South America also contributed to the world treasury of spice. Already around 5000 BC their inhabitants cultivated chillies. The Aztecs made cocoa with allspice and vanilla, and they often put wormwood into their drinks and food.

The knowledge of medicinal plants and spices in Ancient Greece and Rome is related to the name of the philosopher, physician and naturalist, Hippocrates (c. 500 BC). He was an expert on nature and medicine. Some of his humanistic, dietetic and biological principles are still valid. Theophrastos, another naturalist, writes in his treatises 'On the History of Plants' and 'On the Effects of Plants' about spice and medicinal herbs of natural origin, mentioning the healing properties of cinnamon, cassia, thyme, mint, marjoram and pepper. The Greeks greatly valued spices, mainly the imported species, as a symbol of wealth. In the preparation of bread they used home-produced spices such as anise or cumin. Fennel was used in sauces for game; garlic was well known and saffron was served as a seasoning and aphrodisiac, and used as a dye. Other seasonings included coriander, peppermint, parsley, marjoram and thyme. Bay leaf was the holy symbol of the prophetess Pythia and an award for victors and poets.

Alexander the Great deserves the credit for bringing a considerable number of spices into Europe. During his war expeditions to Persia and India, he learned about pepper, cinnamon, mugwort and other oriental spices.

The Greek, Dioscorides, in his work on natural medicinal substances *De materia medica*, (from 100 AD) describes about 600 species of spices and herbs, classifying them in a natural system. His work influenced the medieval herbalists up to about the 16th century. In addition to the already known spices and medicinal herbs, he mentions sage, liquorice and balm. According to his theory, fennel and anise were patent medicines. Another Greek naturalist and physician, Galenos from Pergamon (200 AD), also affected opinions on spice and its healing properties until the 16th century.

The Romans learnt a great deal about spice and its uses from the Greeks. Rare spice (mainly pepper) was brought to Rome from India via Egypt and the Mediterranean. The Romans overestimated the effects of spice so much as to give rise to the saying: 'How strange that a man taking cinnamon dies'. Pliny the Elder, the Roman historian (100 AD), recommended anise which was supposed to make one's breath fragrant, one's face fresher and sleep more easy. According to him, fennel strengthened the eyesight. In his work *Naturalis historia* Pliny mentions pepper, praising it greatly. He claimed that pepper stimulated the appetite and also informs us that the Romans used to nip off young hop sprigs and eat them in a salad with vinegar, salt and pepper.

Garlic and onion were also cultivated but these spices or vegetables were regarded as more suitable for the common people. The Roman, Apicius Caelius, who lived in the reign of Tiberius, wrote the book *De Re Coquinaria* and recommended that food be seasoned with garlic, onion, chives, dill, cumin, fennel, coriander, parsley, saffron, ginger, juniper, bay leaf, pepper, rue, tarragon, mustard, mint, myrtle, sage, savory and thyme. The Lucullian feasts have hardly been surpassed; yet one only has to read 'Trimalchio's Dinner' in Satyricon, where the poet Petronius depicts such an opulent banquet. Pepper was a favourite spice of the Romans and during the decline of the Roman Empire food was highly seasoned; wine too was spiced with mugwort, thyme, mint, myrtle and pine nuts. The Jews praised garlic highly. It is enthusiastically recommended in the Talmud, for 'it nourishes and warms the body, makes a radiant face, multiplies sperms and kills intestinal parasites'.

The Germans, says Diodorus Siculus (100 BC), enjoyed drinking beer, calling it *bior* or *bivor*. They brewed it from barley and seasoned it with hops; a method they had learnt from Finnish tribes. Sorrel was another of their herbs but we have little information about their eating habits.

In the early Middle Ages, the glory of herbs and spices lived on. In the course of the

8th century, under the Frankish king Pepin the Short, cultivation of hops spread over Europe. In the 8th and 9th centuries spices and medicinal herbs, mainly from the Mediterranean area, were cultivated by Benedictine monks in the monasterial gardens. The Benedictine cloisters spread knowledge of the cultivation and use of parsley, dill, hops, mint, horseradish, mustard, etc. The Mother Superior of the Benedictine monastery in Rupersberg on the Rhine in the 12th century, Saint Hildegard, became famous for her extensive knowledge of spices. In her writings she praises horseradish, lovage, marjoram and balm, recommends nutmeg to spice beer and describes savory, hyssop and other spices and herbs from southern Europe and more exotic regions.

Spices were at that time added profusely to everything. The amount of spice was supposed to honour the guest but it was also convenient for masking the flavour of unappetizing meat. The main spices used were exotic pepper, ginger, saffron, cinnamon and nutmeg, used mostly for game at the tables of rich squires. The game was sometimes even sweetened with cane sugar, which was very rare and brought as 'Indian salt' from the crusades in the 11th century, together with pepper, cloves, nutmeg, cardamom, dates, figs, lemons and oranges. The whole of Europe was excited by the reports of the Venetian merchant, Marco Polo, in the 13th century. His book, 'The Million', contains many true and fictitious accounts of spices. He wrote about the islands of Java and Sumatra as sources of nutmeg and clove; he wrote of sesame, pepper, ginger and cinnamon from the Malabar coast. At that time spice was as highly valued as gold.

One of the aims of Columbus's voyages was to reach the Indies and control the spice trade. He never reached the Indies but the ship's doctor, Chanca, brought back paprika pepper, which was not regarded as a spice at the time. It was called Spanish or Indian pepper and at first was considered to be an ornamental plant. Later, however, it spread quickly as a spice and by the 16th century it was a common crop in Germany and Bohemia and, later, in Hungary, where it was regarded as a peasants' spice called 'Turkish pepper'.

The herb basil reached Europe in the 16th century, coming from India. It was reputed to chase away sorrow and melancholia. Marjoram and tarragon also became more popular. Herbaria began to be published, describing both the true and invented effects of spices and drugs. Matthioli's Herbarium from the 16th century is a well-known example, and there are also works by Bock, Fuchs and Tabernaemontanus, based mainly on Dioscorides and Pliny and recommending spice both for food and medicaments.

Matthioli praises nutmeg, anise and fennel. He recommends savory, since 'it endows food with a pleasant and appetizing sharpness, stimulates appetite, promotes digestion, rids of want of appetite and causes liveliness of the body'. He also counsels sage as a seasoning, because 'sundry meals with dry, crushed sage are fragrant and delicious, and wholesome, too'.

In the 16th century, another exotic spice was discovered by the Europeans in Mexico. Francisco Fernandez called it *Piper tabasci* after Tabasco, a Mexican province. The Indians had known it for a long time. It was used in Europe from the 17th century and became extremely popular in England. It was therefore called English spice or pimento or allspice. The 16th century also gave central Europe chives which had been known to both Greeks and Romans. Mugwort, known before but not widely distributed, began to be used in Europe.

In the 16th and 17th centuries, Europeans began to use vanilla brought from Spain and Mexico; Hernan Cortes imported cacao from the Americas.

With the improvement in shipping in the 18th century, spices became more readily available and at a lower price. Developments in science revealed other uses − both medicinal and dietetic − for these tropical spices. Gradually a wide variety of spices was absorbed into the culinary traditions of all the major areas of the world.

The Medicinal Properties
and Uses of Herbs and Spices

There have been a number of arguments about whether it is right or wrong to add spices (particularly the more exotic ones) to food. In fact, the aroma, appearance and taste of food are just as important as the contents. An unattractive-looking meal, even though prepared from first-rate ingredients, will not be properly digested if it is eaten reluctantly. However, large quantities of spice and seasoning should never be used to disguise poor-quality ingredients (as they used to be in the Middle Ages).

Spices and seasoning can be used in a whole range of different combinations – some relatively mild and others extremely pungent. The correct amount of seasoning depends to some extent on the palate of the individual cook and only practice will teach you what suits you.

One of the benefits of using spices and seasonings is that, as well as making you salivate at the appetizing smell in front of you, the aroma also affects the digestive tract so that more juices flow in. This helps to make sure that your food is properly digested. Most herbs and spices will improve your general health but you should not forget the old adage: 'It depends on the dose whether a thing is poisonous or not'.

It is worth remembering that exotic, strongly spiced meals, necessary though they may be in tropical zones, should only be included in a Western diet occasionally. In general, it is better to stick to the principle that each country's cuisine is suited to its climate, the basic ingredients and to its customs.

The Composition of Spices
and Their Effects on the Human Body

Spices usually affect the sense of smell and taste, stimulate the appetite, increase the secretion of gastric juices in the digestive tract, and speed up the intestinal peristalsis, absorption of nutrients from food and the separation and secretion of waste products. Some spices calm the nerves, others stimulate the organism and affect the activity of the heart and kidneys. They contain substances biologically valuable for human health.

Herbs and spices contain a variety of constituents. They comprise *alkaloids* – nitrogenous compounds strongly affecting the physiology of the human body, including potent poisons and efficient medicaments. They are present in pepper, red pepper, poppy, cacao, coffee, tea, angostura bark, love-in-a-mist, mugwort, etc.

Spice also contains *glycosides,* which are derivatives of sugars, mostly with a bitter taste. They are generally poisonous in larger quantities, but their effects vary. They are found, for example, in garlic, mustard, juniper, woodruff, rue, fenugreek, hyssop, saffron, horseradish, capers and mugwort.

15

Other components are *essential oils,* which are intensely aromatic, volatile, oleaginous liquids. They used to be known as *etheric oils.* They mostly occur in the form of terpenes and their compounds, and are found in all the exotic and domestic species, for example, in mint, thyme, marjoram, balm, savory, hyssop, as well as in juniper, fennel, hops, cumin, horseradish, lovage, red pepper, parsley, lemon rind, cinnamon and many others. Some essential oils affect the nerves, others promote the flow of gastric juices or improve the appetite, others intensify the circulation of the blood, act as a disinfectant, carminative or diuretic.

Spices also contain *mucilages* which are susceptible to swelling and consequently affect the mucous membranes by covering and protecting them. They are found, for example, in borage, mugwort, fenugreek and cinnamon.

Tannins are related to glycosides. They are non-nitrogenous substances with an astringent taste. Herbs containing tannins, for example hyssop, basil, oregano, rosemary, savory, marjoram, should not be cooked too long. Tannins also decompose in the air so these herbs should be stored in airtight containers. They exert antibacterial and antiviral action, and stop haemorrhages and diarrhoea.

Fats are also present in spices – mostly in seeds and nuts of various types, which have to be protected from light and heat which cause decomposition of fats. Oils are found in olives, mustard seeds, fenugreek, fennel, star anise, pepper and nutmeg, for example.

Glycides and *proteins* are also constituents of spices. Those rich in glycides include cinnamon, ginger, fennel seeds, pepper seeds, fruits of orange, rowan and juniper. Seeds of fenugreek have a high percentage of proteins, as well as yeast.

Resins form in some plants as a product of metabolism. In spices, they are present in turmeric, angelica, galangal, hyssop, asafetida, love-in-a-mist, rue, sage, and thyme.

Organic acids occur in fruits and foliage (lemon, orange, pomegranate, raisins, sorrel, sumach, rowanberries, juniper berries, ground ivy, barberries and Cornelian cherries). They have a slightly sour taste and light purgative properties.

Bitter principles are non-nitrogenous, non-poisonous bitter substances stimulating the appetite. They exist in southernwood, mugwort, tarragon, hops, lavender, sweet flag, rue, marjoram, ground ivy, thyme, ginger, etc.

Saponins are substances which can be toxic in large doses. In small quantities, they have a faintly irritant effect on the mucous membranes of the alimentary tract, and have diuretic and slightly purgative effects. They are contained in love-in-a-mist, borage, fenugreek, thyme and liquorice.

Phytoncides can destroy germs (viruses, bacteria or fungi), even in tiny quantities. They are chemically non-unified substances which are still under research. They do not lose their value in the drying process. Some of them have an anthelmintic effect. They are present in onion, garlic, horseradish, nettles, coriander, rosemary, southernwood and wild thyme, and can be found in juniper berries, hops, mustard, thyme and others.

Minerals are also important, mainly potassium and calcium, but also sodium, iodine and sulphur. Sulphur is found in onion and garlic, iodine in tarragon, and manganese in borage. Onions and garlic contain large quantities of potassium and phosphorus. Iron and magnesium are found mainly in the green shoots. Horseradish, for example, contains a lot of potassium, sodium and magnesium, as well as calcium and sulphur. Salts of sodium are found in dandelions, and nettles contain a lot of potassium and calcium.

Fresh green herbs contain *vitamins,* which are indispensable for the functioning of the human body: above all vitamin C, provitamin and vitamin A, and the B group vitamins and others. The amounts of these decrease with the drying process. Dried yeast is rich in B vitamins. Vitamin C is found in the greenery of parsley, hyssop, chives, onion and nasturtium, and in other herbs used in their green form. Good sources of vitamin C are the fruits of sea buckthorn, hips, rowanberries, lemons, oranges, etc.

Of considerable importance is the presence of *ferments* (enzymes) in every living plant. They act as biocatalysts. It is therefore very healthy to eat fresh green shoots or fresh fruits of certain plants used as spices. Ferments promote digestion and accelerate metabolism.

Furocoumarins are present in roots, fruits and seeds of plants of the families Lamiaceae and Daucaceae. They form a component of essential oils, have antispasmodic effects, and help to regulate the metabolism.

Achillea millefolium

Substances with hormonal effects. In the human body, these substances of vegetable origin act as biocatalysts, similarly to animal hormones. They are found in hops, anise, sage, pepper polygonum, rowanberries, nasturtium, onion, liquorice and fenugreek.

Vegetal pigments not only produce colour in plants, but are also important in other ways for their survival. They have numerous effects on the human body — for example, the pigment chlorophyll (from the green parts of plants) is an antibiotic and removes odour — such as bad breath as a result of eating garlic. Chlorophyll is found in abundance in the leaves of nettle, sorrel and parsley and in other herbs. It complements carotene and xantophyll (yellow and red pigments). Carotene is the provitamin A, which is transformed in the body into vitamin A. Anthocyanins are the red to blue pigments of flowers, fruits and leaves. Some of them favourably affect the regeneration of the iris pigments. Pigments of turmeric are successfully used to treat gall bladder diseases.

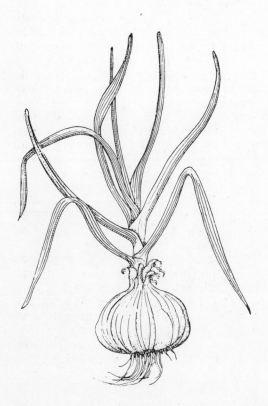

Allium cepa

18

Flavonoides reduce fragility of the capillaries. They are present in red pepper, juniper berries, hyssop, wild thyme, crispated mint, liquorice and pepper polygonum, for example.

Spices in Folk Medicine

Some spices have healing effects, but the amount used in kitchen seasoning is too weak to produce any pronounced results. They are usually obtained by specific doses and preparation. Sage, hyssop and ginger, for instance, inhibit excessive sweating. Some spices, such as red pepper, stimulate the cardiac muscle, while others, such as wormwood, sea buckthorn, hops, mint, poppy, balm, rose, woodruff, bay leaf, dill, relax the nervous system. Some prevent arteriosclerosis (garlic and rue) or reduce hypertension (garlic and hops), others act as expectorants and reliev coughs (ground ivy, hyssop, poppy, thyme and wild thyme). Nutmeg, mace and balm are beneficial for an impaired nervous system.

Certain spices affect the appetite and promote the gastric function; they are mostly plants from the family Lamiaceae (balm, mints and wild marjoram), but also wormwood, angelica, red pepper, horseradish, pepper, nutmeg and mace, woodruff, liquorice, and others.

Many spices relieve flatulence and spasms of the intestinal tract, and prevent the formation of gas; these include cumin, coriander, fennel, marjoram, anise, savory, balm, mint, basil, ginger, nutmeg and mace.

Diarrhoea provoked by fatty food can be checked by garlic, thyme, hyssop, ground ivy, savory, marjoram, saxifrage, sage, oregano, mint, balm and sumach. Some herbs have a cathartic action and affect the peristalsis of the large intestine: they include pectins and organic acids, present mainly in oranges, lemons, rowanberries and so on.

Other spices promote the secretion of bile and the function of the gall bladder and related organs. Unless the gall bladder is inflamed, it is a good idea to season heavy meals with horseradish, mustard, wormwood or mugwort. The secretion of the gall bladder is affected by rosemary, barberries, mint, juniper berries, nasturtium and turmeric, and they should be added to fatty meals.

Spices can act as a diuretic and help to eliminate noxious substances from the body. In this respect hops, borage, barberries, juniper berries, lovage, parsley, saxifrage, nutmeg and mace are to be recommended. Savory stimulates the pancreas.

Fresh rue (in small quantities), parsley leaves, thyme, wild thyme, cloves, allspice, coriander and anise can be used to treat bad breath and they also have deodorant properties.

The tiredness most people feel after a long winter can be prevented by wild herbs — such as chives, nasturtium, lady's smock, garlic species, nettles, sorrel, leaves of English daisies and milfoil, violets and other green herbs.

Some spices have been described in folk medicine as aphrodisiacs — pepper, celery and parsley leaves, peppermint, vanilla, savory and others. On the other hand, some, such as hops and dill, reduce sexual excitability.

There are spices which could adversely affect pregnancy and should not be taken in large doses at this time. These include rue, rosemary, love-in-a-mist, pepper polygonum, pepper, cinnamon and juniper.

Herbs and Spices in Diet

In the course of certain diseases, some spices should be avoided. Persons suffering from stomach ulcers should not use pepper, but can safely use savory instead. In the case of kidney inflammation, juniper berries should not be used. With gastric trouble, ginger, allspice, clove, all species of hot peppers, hot mustard, horseradish, too much garlic, onion, nutmeg, mace, and larger doses of bay leaves should be avoided.

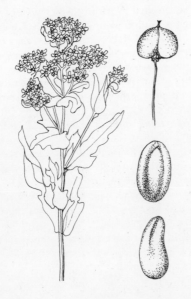

Lepidium sativum

Good flavour and aroma are particularly important in dietetic cooking. Monotonous and insipid food and the patients' lack of appetite can be improved by using fragrant herbs. Moderate doses of fresh or dried parsley, mint, savory, basil, hyssop, thyme, oregano, balm, fresh chives and so on can make the diet more appetizing.

The use of a suitable spice substitute is essential in diets which forbid salt. In cardiac diseases the intake of salt, lemon rind and yeast should be reduced, as should curry, ginger, bay leaf, mace, vanilla, cinnamon, red pepper (which should only be taken in very small quantities) and herbs and seasonings such as basil, savory, dill, borage, tarragon, parsley, cumin, marjoram, thyme, chives, balm, chervil, coriander and mushrooms. The doctor's advice should always be followed.

Growing and Preparing Herbs

Certain rules should always be followed for the successful cultivation, collection and drying of herbs:

1. Choose the right season for collecting; time of day is also significant in the case of some species, including mint (at night some plants do not produce the right active constituents and the taste of the herb will not be as strong as it might). In general, it is best to pick herbs in the early morning.
2. Pick only well-developed, healthy plants. Plants affected by disease may well be dangerous to eat.
3. Use scissors when cutting off leaves and stems and, when you have finished collecting, never store herbs in plastic bags.
4. Make sure the collected parts of the plants are completely clean. Avoid collecting near busy main roads, for the plants may well have absorbed fumes from car exhausts.
5. Never dry your herbs in direct sunlight as this will lead to the evaporation of the essential oils. Lay the plants in a thin layer on wooden frames in a room with gently circulating air. Finish the drying process with moderate artificial heat.

Pick Your Own Pot-herbs

Many wild plants, which for centuries formed part of our ancestors' diet, have maintained their importance today. Most wild herbs and flowers contain substances which are beneficial to human health: minerals, vitamins, etc., while the leaves, flowers, fruits or roots of others are simply used as flavouring.

Sweet Violet *(Viola odorata)*

Sweet Violet is well-known for its fragrant flowers and its leaves can be added to herb soups. Violet flowers are sometimes candied and used for cake decoration, or flavoured with vinegar.

Hoary Cress *(Lepidium draba)*

Hoary Cress is a perennial plant with rich panicles of white flowers. Its distribution is almost world-wide, and it thrives in warm areas. Hoary Cress seeds can be used as an alternative to pepper as a condiment, as they have a similarly peppery taste.

Taraxacum officinale

Ribwort *(Plantago lanceolata)*
Ribwort grows in grassy areas, near woods and on hillsides. It is reputed to have medicinal properties: it contains constituents affecting digestion, regulating the bowels and acting as an expectorant. Young Ribwort leaves can be added to herb soups and to sauces; chopped leaves may be mixed into pancake batters and omelettes or fried in a sweet batter as a dessert.

Herb Bennet *(Geum urbanum)*
Herb Bennet is a perennial plant with an undivided rhizome, up to 2 cm (3/4in) thick. The five-lobed yellow flowers are small and inconspicuous. It grows in shrubberies, woodland, and on waste ground. The dried rootstock contains essential oils and smells of clove and cinnamon. Herb Bennet is used as a seasoning and may also be added to mulled wine and liqueurs. It can be used as substitute for cloves or cinnamon.

Dandelion *(Taraxacum officinale)*
A common weed, Dandelion has both dietetic and medicinal uses. The boiled root (taken from a plant in spring, before blossoming time), administered in small doses, has biliary and diuretic effects, stimulating digestion. It contains insulin, the glycoside which helps to treat diabetes. Fresh young Dandelion leaves are said to stimulate the metabolism and reduce blood pressure. They can be picked till May. The French eat Dandelion leaves as a salad, with a vinaigrette dressing, and the leaves can also be added, in small quantities, to soups and sauces.

Milfoil *(Achillea millefolium)*
Milfoil grows wild in dry meadows and on hillsides. Its flowers are white or pink, and form small rosettes. Young Milfoil, used in small quantities, makes a spicy, bitter-sweet seasoning for soups and stews. Milfoil is said to relax intestinal spasms, stimulate the circulation of the blood and the secretion of the gastric juices. It is also said to alleviate coughing and to have healing and disinfectant properties.

Lady's Smock *(Cardamine pratensis)*
Lady's Smock grows in humid meadows and can be anything from 10 to 50 cm (4 to 20in) high. It has a rosette of basal leaves on the stalk and white or pale violet flowers which appear from April to June. Only the basal leaves, which have a pleasantly sharp taste, should be eaten. Lady's Smock is said to promote digestion and to act as a diuretic. Rich in vitamins, the leaves can be used to flavour cheese spreads and potato salads.

Daisy *(Bellis perennis)*
(also known as **Bachelor's Button)**
Depending on the weather, Daisies flower from February to November, and some-times even into December. The basal rosettes of leaves and buds should be harvested in spring. As well as containing vitamins, the Daisy contains substances with anti-inflammatory effects, and which relieve coughing. It can be used in salads and herb soups.

How to Store Herbs and Spices

The way spices should be stored depends on the ingredients of individual spices.

Spices containing fats, nutmeg and mustard for example, must not be stored in transparent containers in daylight. Both light and air turn the fats rancid and destroy their flavour. Instead, they should be kept in dark, airtight receptacles, stored in a cool, dry, dark place. Likewise, spices containing volatile essential oils should not be kept in containers with loose lids.

Transparent containers in daylight will make the green parts of plants turn greyish. Your spice shelf should never hang directly above a stove, because the steam and heat will reduce the quality of the spices. Humidity in the room can also destroy spices by making them turn mouldy.

Spice containers should therefore not just be pretty; they should also be functional. Wide-mouthed bottles of dark glass and with ground plugs are highly recommended, and ceramic containers with well-fitting lids are also suitable. Old-fashioned tiny drawers and decorative boxes with loose lids are totally inappropriate for storing ground spice or spice from the Lamiaceae family. Most containers with screw caps or well-fitting lids are suitable, provided they are not made of clear plastic. Wooden boxes are attractive containers and, if the lids are well turned, the spice will not lose its fragrance or flavour. As the wood will absorb the odour of the spice, the same box must always be used for the same spice.

Any spice which is freshly ground in a small mill or grinder, grated on a tiny grater or crushed in a porcelain, wooden or metal mortar, is more aromatic and piquant than one bought ready-ground. But for the occasions when time is short, it is useful to have a small quantity of ground spice ready. Similarly, when preparing mixed spices, never make too large a quantity, and store it in an airtight container, only slightly bigger than the amount of the mixture.

Equipment

An essential item for grinding spices is a good mortar and pestle, preferably of wood rather than metal. A porcelain mortar and pestle will also quickly pulverize any spice, dry or fresh, including garlic and onion. It is advisable to choose a reasonably big mortar so that it can be used for crushing the larger seeds and fruits, and dry herbs, either into a fine or coarse-grained mixture, depending on the recipe.

A spice mill or grinder is also essential. It can be adjusted according to the desired coarseness of the spice. Pepper is particularly aromatic when freshly ground, as is cumin.

A small grater with tiny perforations is also extremely useful — nutmeg, in particular, is best when freshly grated, otherwise it loses its aroma. The grater may also be used equally for lemon or orange rind, ginger, or turmeric.

Hints for Herbalists

If you have never tasted a meal seasoned with freshly picked and chopped herbs, you should try it next spring. You will be amazed at what a delicious, healthy dish can be made from simple, fresh ingredients. If you have a garden, no matter how small, you can grow your own herbs. Some herbs, including hyssop, rosemary, perennial savory, marjoram, lavender and rue can even be grown in a rockery, provided it is in a sunny place. Other herbs prefer partial shade (lovage, horseradish, chives and mint, for example). Herbs will even grow on a balcony or on a window-sill: chives, balm, lovage, borage, savory, marjoram and sage all do well in window boxes. Others can be grown in pots, basil, rosemary, thyme and dill amongst them. Garden cress is one of the easiest to grow – it only needs a shallow plastic box lined with damp cotton wool, in order to germinate. If it is put near a window, at room temperature, it will grow in a week, even in winter.

Ideally, any cook should aim to grow a selection of the following herbs for use in the kitchen: lovage, tarragon, rue, lavender, rosemary, hyssop, mountain savory, perennial marjoram and thyme. All these herbs, except perhaps for lovage and tarragon, look pretty in a rockery or in a flower bed. For a continuous supply, you should aim to grow five to ten plants each of the following: garden savory, chives, borage, basil, probably sage, oregano, fennel, horseradish, celery and coriander. You will need 10 to 20 plants or more of peppermint, woodruff, marjoram, balm and portulaca.

You should sow a row 1 m (1yd) long of dill seeds so that every month you have a few young plants available, and if you like borage, do the same with that, and perhaps with parsley and Welsh onions.

If you live in a flat, you can grow fresh rootstalks of ginger in pots, or you could try lemon grass. When growing herbs in a garden keep the annuals in one place and the perennials in another. Some of the less hardy species of herbs should be started indoors in a box (or in a hot bed or greenhouse). They should only be transplanted after the spring frosts are over. These herbs include basil, marjoram, balm, red pepper, celery, rue, sage, thyme and hyssop. More delicate plants such as chervil, fennel and coriander can be sown directly outside in late April, as they suffer from transplanting and only grow well when sown directly into the soil. They should therefore be sown where they are to be harvested. This group also includes chervil, dill, borage, garden cress, fennel, coriander, parsley, savory, hyssop, balm and chives.

While the young plants are growing they should be watered and the ground weeded. The tops and leaves are harvested and used fresh.

When herbs are to be dried, they should be collected just before flowering, except for a few which are picked at the flowering stage (dill, basil, hyssop, savory, portulaca among them).

Herbs and Spices and World Cookery

The cookery of a nation is based, above all, on local ingredients, and is characterized by traditions and customs related to the climate, history, way of life and distribution of natural resources of that country. National cooking styles have existed for a long time – for example, the Islamic invasions of centuries ago have resulted in easily identified modes of food preparation which stretch today from India, across the south-eastern Soviet Union to the Balkans. Today, many once purely national dishes have become part of so-called international cooking; curry is a good example of this – curry powders or pastes are now used throughout the world; some Chinese specialities have also become popular – sweet and sour pork, for example, now appears on menus from California to Greece. But this trend towards international cooking has provoked a contrary desire in many people for traditional, genuinely national dishes using local materials and traditional combinations of ingredients.

African Cooking

Although Africa does not boast such variety of food as, for instance, Asia, African dishes seem highly exotic and unusual, especially to Europeans.

In North Africa and other Muslim parts of the continent, the local food is related to Arab cooking. Much use is made of mutton, pulses, fresh and dried vegetables, exotic fruits, and aromatics and spices.

During the last half century, the eating habits of African city dwellers have become increasingly international. In the African bush, however, things are totally different. Here meat is generally either boiled or open-roasted. Staples include crushed maize and of course the legendary 'fufu' – pounded cassava served with a hot, spicy vegetable stew. Plants are gathered to complement the meagre diet, while palm wine is still a favourite drink.

In East Africa, in Ethiopia, 'Berbera', a mixture of crushed chillies and herbs (dried cow's bile is also sometimes added) is used as an extremely sharp, but appetizing condiment.

Arab Cooking

Arab cooking is closely related to the Muslim faith, for the Koran prohibits alcoholic drinks and pork as unclean. Lamb and goat meat are therefore extremely popular and, instead of alcohol, spiced tea and coffee are widely consumed; vegetables, rise and pulses, all heavily spiced, help supplement the diet. From the civilizations of Greece and Rome the Arabs inherited their taste for fat meat, strong spices and excessively sweet dishes; from the ancient Egyptians, they adopted the use of onions, garlic and leeks.

Contemporary Arab cooking includes many dishes which originated in south-east Asia, in India, Iran, the Balkans and North Africa. Variations of pilaf and kebabs exist as far away as Pakistan; and both the famous Moroccan pastilla, which originated in the Maghreb during the Moorish invasion, and couscous, that spicy meat stew served with semolina (originally a Berber dish), are now popular throughout the Arab world.

Most Middle Eastern meat dishes feature a hot sauce seasoned with pepper, cinnamon, chilli peppers, onion, garlic, mint, nutmeg, ginger and saffron. The spices are usually first blended in powder or paste form. And no Arab's meal would be complete without the oversweet dessert-pastries stuffed with sugar, nuts and honey, spiced with cinnamon and filled with figs, almonds and raisins — baklava, kadaifi and the others.

The characteristic aroma of a Moroccan kitchen is of mint leaves, rose water, olives and oriental spices. In Tunisia, ginger and pepper predominate, with herbs like mint, rosemary, balm, dill and sage; fish and seafood are extremely popular in Syria and the Lebanon. Many Arab stews are cooked in sesame oil and sour milk and in Jordan, highly seasoned camel meat is considered a great delicacy.

Chinese Cooking

For the rich and powerful of ancient China, classic cooking was one of life's aesthetic pleasures: even the ancient poets admired the creations of Chinese chefs and the cooking and preparation of culinary *chefs d'oeuvres* was respected as an art form. Chinese dishes were praised then for their exquisite taste, aroma, colour and consistency. In addition, according to the ancient philosopher Confucius, they had to be in harmony with the seasons of the year. By judicious combination of taste, colour and aroma, with one of these characteristics predominating in each dish, one may reach the desired result. Yet it is important, as Confucius said, 'not to overcook or undercook the food: do not cut it or season in inappropriately'. Stir-frying evolved a technique of fast yet thorough cooking which meant that Confucius' advice was followed. Today, rice or flour-and-water pancakes form the basis of the average Chinese diet. The staple ingredient is usually served with some meat and vegetables and seasoned with soy sauce and other seasonings and spices.

French Cooking

While local French dishes may vary greatly from region to region, they remain related by a delicate network, a highly sophisticated yet broad spectrum of flavourings ranging from exotic spices to fresh or dried home-grown herbs.

Spices imported into France include black and white pepper, cloves, ginger, nutmeg, mace, cinnamon and allspice, chilli peppers, cayenne and sweet peppers. Home-grown herbs, including bay leaf, thyme and parsley are combined to form the famous 'bouquet garni', a small bunch of herbs tied up in muslin and added to soups and casserole dishes. Aromatics — tarragon, chives, chervil, fennel leaves, marjoram, wild thyme, rosemary, dill, basil, sage, savory, mint, oregano, hyssop — all are now basic to French cooking.

Many types of onion are also commonly used, including garlic, shallots and rocambole. Garlic is, of course, a must for any French cook and is most widely used in the south, in Provence, where the delicious garlic mayonnaise, aïoli, has justly become world famous.

Other spices and flavourings used in French cooking include saffron (again, mainly used in the south), fennel, juniper and horseradish; nuts are also used in various dishes. Seasoned and spiced wine and fruit vinegars are also popular, as are spiced mustards.

Truffles, hot-bed field agarics, sharp or orange agarics and other mushrooms are still often used for seasoning sauces, although their cost is becoming increasingly prohibitive. The use of wine or other alcohol is also typical of French cooking and there are few soups, sauces or flambé dishes that cannot be improved by the addition of a little wine, cider, brandy or calvados.

Indian Cooking

Curry, the undisputed king of Indian cooking, is both the name of a spice mixture and the description of a whole family of dishes containing, in varying proportions, a whole battery of spices and herbs.

While ready-made curry powder, a prepared mixture of several spices, is most often used by Europeans for curries, in India cooks mix their own spices, to a powder or paste, effectively creating an individual, unique taste and aroma each time they cook.

Various fanciful combinations of spices are essential to the quality of Indian dishes. Common spices include coriander, ginger, turmeric, garlic, onion, asafoetida, basil, cardamom, cinnamon, aniseed, cloves, cumin, nutmeg and chillies.

Not all Indian dishes need be hot: pepper, chillies and other strong, fiery flavourings are usually added towards the end of cooking time, according to personal taste.

South American Cooking

As with other tropical areas of the world, South American food is characterized by pronounced hot seasoning, in this case that of chilli peppers.

It was the South American Indians who taught the new settlers, the Conquistadors, how to make their native dishes and how to cultivate their plants. In their turn, the Spaniards enriched the native South American cooking with their own customs and techniques. Later, in the early 19th century, workers from India and China brought curry powder and soy sauce to the Caribbean Antilles Islands and taught the islanders how to use fresh and dried ginger. Today, spicy oils are used to cook the meat, saffron and garlic and pepper are used in stews, and brown sugar and fruit are often added to meat dishes. Hibiscus blossom, orange rind and juice, cinnamon and cloves are all used to flavour exotic fruit drinks and punches.

Nowadays, all Spanish-speaking Latin American cooks prepare dishes similar to those of mainland Spain. They use a lot of oregano, onion, garlic, tomatoes, red peppers and chillies, ginger, cumin, coriander, dried and fresh mace, nutmeg, allspice, cinnamon, saffron, cloves and plenty of aromatic herbs, particularly thyme.

Italian Cooking

Today's Italian food is directly descended from the cooking of ancient Rome and, indeed, some of the old Roman dishes are still being produced in their original form in today's Italy.

Italian food is more heavily spiced than French food, and onions and garlic are used

28

to the full; Italian olive oil gives the food a characteristic, spicy fragrance. Aromatic herbs, many of them growing in the wild, form the basis of Italian seasoning. One cannot imagine an Italian tomato sauce without basil; parsley and chives are ubiquitous; oregano gives the right touch to meat-filled pasta dishes; wild marjoram, with its slightly different flavour, is widely used in sauces; thyme is used to flavour beef; sage spices veal, lamb, fish and tripe and is often used to enhance the flavour of roast pork; fresh mint is used in salad dressings and with artichokes; savory, bay leaves, borage, aniseed and fennel are also used to the full. Italian food is often additionally flavoured with black or green olives, with capers, pistachio nuts, pine nuts and raisins. On occasion, orange blossom may be used to add fragrance to a dessert.

As in French cooking, the use of wine in meat or poultry dishes is widespread.

North American Cooking

North American cooking, especially in the countryside, has its origins not only in the traditions of the immigrant English-speaking settlers in the north and the Spanish-speaking ones in the south, but also from racial minorities, not least from the traditions of the American negro and the Indian.

While the use of spices in North American cooking is subtler than in the south, it nevertheless performs an important role in the cooking of the USA. In particular, sage, thyme, savory, fresh parsley, mint, chervil, marjoram, cloves, pepper, cayenne, allspice, cinnamon, paprika, nutmeg, coriander and mustard are used.

In the deep south the food is hotter and spicier — a legacy from the Spanish and also related to the proximity of Mexico. The states of Texas, New Mexico and Arizona are known for more exotic spice combinations — the heavy use of garlic, oregano, cumin, ginger, coriander, sage and, above all, chilli peppers.

A typical American meal of today might well include grilled meat, served with 'barbecue sauce' which can be bought in concentrated form or as a powdered mixture; this sauce is always hot and sometimes sweetish, often containing fruit of some kind.

The Cooking of the Soviet Union

Russian peasant food is characterized by substantial dishes, thick meat, fish and vegetable soups such as *borshcht, shchi* and *solyanka* which are eaten as a meal in themselves. Cabbage, beetroot, turnips, radishes, onions, fennel and dill are common ingredients in Russian cooking. Yet something still remains of the French influence on Russian food, dating from the era when French chefs used to cook at courts of the nobility.

Caucasian-style food makes the most of herbs, which often grow wild in the region itself. Influenced also by eastern cooking, Caucasians use lots of coriander seed, cinnamon, cardamom, saffron, aniseed, cloves, ginger, chilli peppers and tropical fruits. *Shashlik* (grilled lamb on skewers), the most famous dish from the Caucasus, is sprinkled with dried cornelian berries, barberries, sea buckthorn and sumach. *Adjika* is a hot, Armenian spice paste containing garlic, coriander, vinegar, dill, ground fresh paprika and salt.

29

In the far north of the country, Siberian cooking also has its own distinct character; game is widely eaten, seasoned with a marvellous combination of wild garlic and hot agarics.

Spanish and Portuguese Cooking
Herbs and spices are both widely used in Spain and Portugal, their cooking traditions affected by Moorish influence and by the importation of exotic spices from the Far East, centuries ago. Most commonly used herbs and spices include oregano, thyme, wild marjoram, mint, dill, tarragon, sage, rosemary, hyssop, chervil, basil, chilli peppers and cayenne pepper; onions and garlic are ever-present. The direct influence of the Moors is apparent in the use of raisins and almonds in savoury dishes and the seasoning of spinach with nutmeg.

Two colours predominate in the cooking of Spain and Portugal, yellow and red, the colours of paprika and saffron. Other widely used seasonings include pepper, nutmeg, mace and cinnamon. Chocolate is sometimes added to hot, spicy meat sauces.

British Cooking
British cookery has always laid stress on the high quality of materials — beef, lamb, pork, fish — all of which are available in quantity as well as quality.

Since medieval times English cooks have been adept at pickling and preserving and, with the advent of the spice trade and world travel, new and exciting materials were introduced to supplement native ingredients.

Today English food is still generously seasoned with both spices and aromatics — pepper, nutmeg, ginger, cayenne, fennel, marjoram, bay leaves, cloves, thyme, sage, savory, rosemary, basil, cress, parsley, mint, mustard, tarragon, onions and garlic — all are currently used to add flavour to traditional or imported dishes.

Mixed Herbs, Spices and Condiments

Ready-made herb and spice mixtures exist in a plentiful assortment but every gourmet, when cooking at leisure, prefers to try and make up his own special mixture. Here are several kinds of spice mixture which are suitable for specific types of dishes. Once you have experimented with these, you can let your imagination run free.

Cardamine pratensis

Mixed spices for soups

Ragout mixture
(Suitable for ragout-type dishes using creamed veal or chicken and soups)
2 parts ground edible boletus
1 part ground mace
1 part ground nutmeg
1/2 part ground ginger

Bouquet garni
(Excellent for meat consommés, vegetable and meat stews)
1 bay leaf
1 clove garlic
sprig or pinch thyme
several sprigs parsley

Soup mixture
(Good for consommés and cream soups)
30g (1oz) black pepper
10g (1/4oz) white pepper
5g (pinch) ground nutmeg
2 ground bay leaves
5g (pinch) thyme
5g (pinch) cloves
20g (3/4oz) ginger
5g (pinch) ground mace
Season 1 litre (2 pints) of soup with 1/4 to 1/2 teaspoon of the pulverized mixture.
Store in an airtight container.

Simple consommé mixture
2 berries allspice
2 peppercorns
1/2 bay leaf
pinch thyme
1 clove garlic, crushed
This is sufficient for 1 litre (2 pints) of consommé.

Mixed spices for roast meat

Sage mixture
2 parts dry sage
1 part each of ground allspice, pepper, cloves, ginger, dry lemon rind
Pulverize and mix and sprinkle over meat, or dip bacon rashers in it if larding the meat.

Marjoram mixture
2 parts marjoram
1/2 part each of ground nutmeg, ground mace, ground ginger

Mixed spices for chopped or minced meat

Thyme mixture
2 parts thyme
1 part each of lemon rind, ground allspice, ground cloves, black pepper, ground ginger
Crush in a mortar and mix.

Marjoram mixture
2 parts marjoram
1 part each of ground nutmeg, ground ginger, ground mace, pepper, ground cloves

Italian seasoning
(Used for hamburgers, risotto, spaghetti sauce, pizzas, stewed meat with tomatoes)
Equal parts of: oregano, thyme, savory, sage, rosemary, basil, ground pepper
Pulverize and mix.

Indian seasoning
Equal parts of: black pepper, ground cinnamon, ground cloves, ground cardamom, crushed garlic

Indian seasoning for meat balls
Equal quantities of: ground cinnamon, ground cloves, ground coriander, chilli pepper

Mexican spice mixture
(Used for chilli con carne)
Equal parts of: chilli pepper, sage, garlic, ground cumin, ground coriander, oregano

Fresh herb mixtures

Use only fresh herbs, chopped very finely, according to taste.

Canapé mixture
Equal parts of:
1 chervil, parsley, chives, celery leaves
2 tarragon, parsley, chives
3 hyssop, parsley, balm
4 chives, parsley, hyssop
5 dill, chives, borage

Salad mixture
Equal parts of:
1 chervil, parsley, tarragon
2 cress, parsley
3 borage, parsley, savory
4 dill, parsley, mint
5 rosemary, garlic, onion
6 basil, garlic, parsley
7 parsley, mint, dill, sage, hyssop, rosemary, basil, balm

Herbal soup mixture
Equal parts of: violet, ground ivy, strawberry, clover, dandelion, nettle, wild chives, ribwort, wild garlic, lovage, parsley

Vegetable soup mixture
Equal parts of: lovage, parsley, thyme, savory, celery leaves, basil

Mixed spices for grilled meat

The following mixtures can be used for grilled meat, either spread on to the meat directly or mixed into a paste with a small quantity of oil, and then rubbed into the meat. All mixtures are of equal parts of ingredients.

Barbecue mixtures
1 Sweet pepper, chillies, onion powder or juice, celery leaves, ground nutmeg, garlic powder, juice or crushed garlic, oregano, ground allspice, ground coriander, mustard powder, sage, ground caraway, ground cloves, pepper, salt, monosodium glutamate
2 Red pepper, curry powder, grated garlic and onion, monosodium glutamate
3 Thyme, sage, savory, pepper, grated onion
4 Ground ginger, parsley, grated onion and garlic
5 Curry powder, parsley, grated onion and garlic, minced mixed vegetables, monosodium glutamate

Herbal mixture for grilled meat (fresh or dry herbs can be used)
Equal parts of garlic (crushed), rosemary, basil, oregano
1/2 part each of sage, peppermint, thyme, pepper
Blend with garlic and oil.

Mixed spice for paté or game

1 part each ground black pepper, ground allspice. 1/2 part each thyme, cloves
   1 large bay leaf
2 Equal parts of cloves, nutmeg, mace, peppers, thyme, basil, bay leaf (pulverize)

3 Equal parts of white pepper, blade pepper, ground allspice, ground cloves, ground mace, thyme, marjoram, basil, rosemary, red pepper, ginger, nutmeg, bay leaves

Curry mixtures

Equal parts of the following, all ground:
1 Cardamom, cloves, mace, nutmeg, cinnamon, cumin, pepper
2 Chilli, coriander, turmeric, cumin, fennel, mustard
3 Coriander, black pepper, fennel, poppy, ginger, chilli, caraway
4 Turmeric, ginger, cayenne pepper, caraway, coriander, black pepper, cardamom, cloves

Georgian mixture
(For stews, vegetables and minced meats)
Equal parts of: coriander, dill, celery, parsley, basil, savory, mint, bay leaf
1/2 part each of saffron and rosemary

Geum urbanum

Seasoned oils

If spices or other ingredients are marinated in oil for several days, the oil will have a spicy aroma and taste. The following mixtures can be made for different types of dishes.

Fish salad oil
1/2 litre (2 pints) oil
50g (2oz) parsley root
50g (2 oz) celery
Pinch thyme, lemon rind and allspice
1 bay leaf
Heat the oil up to 80°C and marinate for 2 days in a cool, dark place. Strain the oil and use in salads.

Red pepper oil
Marinate chopped fresh chillies (or milder red pepper pods if preferred, cut into thin strips) in good-quality oil for several days, covered, in a cool, dark place. Strain the oil and use for seasoning and for Chinese dishes. The drained peppers can be used in salads or cooked dishes.

Ginger oil
Peel fresh ginger root and cut into slices. Marinate in good quality oil 3 to 4 days in a cool, dark place. Strain and use the oil for salads and for Indian dishes.

Garlic oil
Fry 4 chopped cloves of garlic in 200 ml (1/3 pint) oil heated to 80°C. Leave in a cool, dark place for a few days and strain. Use the oil in salads.

Aromatized vinegars
Wine or fruit vinegars can be aromatized and used in salads, sauces, and mayonnaises.

Tarragon vinegar
You will need 100g (4oz) tarragon (approximately one shoot of the plant) for every litre (2 pints) vinegar. Cover and marinate for 2 weeks in a cool, dark place. Strain.

Apple vinegar
Use 100g (4oz) apple, unpeeled and finely chopped, to every litre (2 pints) of vinegar. Marinate as above and strain.

Bay leaf vinegar
You will need 5 big bay leaves for every litre (2 pints) vinegar. Marinate as for tarragon vinegar and strain.

Herbal vinegar — 1
You will need 100g (4oz) mixed tarragon, balm, lime flowers, maraschino cherry leaves, bay leaves to every litre (2 pints) of vinegar. Marinate as for tarragon vinegar, and strain.

Herbal vinegar — 2
For every litre (2 pints) vinegar you will need a handful of fresh tarragon leaves, 1 chilli, 1 medium-sized onion (sliced), 3 sprigs chervil or parsley, 1 small elderflower-head, 6 peppercorns. Marinate as for tarragon vinegar and strain.

Herbal vinegar — 3
You will need 100g (4oz) fresh herbs and fruits (basil, red currant, sprigs of wild thyme, balm and tarragon) for every litre (2 pints) vinegar. Marinate as for tarragon vinegar, strain and use in salads.

Violet vinegar
For every litre (2 pints) vinegar take a handful of violet flowers. Marinate for 10 days in a cool, dark place and strain.

Red currant vinegar
You will need 1/4 to 1/2 kg (1/2 to 1 lb) red currants (crushed) for every litre (2 pints) vinegar. Marinate for a week in a cool, dark place and strain. Boil it to make it keep. It can be added to lemonade.

Lemon or orange vinegar
Cut the rind of 4 lemons (or oranges) and add to a litre (2 pints) of vinegar. Marinate as for tarragon vinegar and strain. Do not use chemically treated fruit.

Lemon vinegar
Add 4 peeled and sliced lemons, plus the rind of 1 lemon, to 500ml (1 pint) of wine vinegar. Marinate for 5 days in a cool, dark place and strain.

Balm vinegar
You will need 100g (4oz) balm leaves for every litre (2 pints) of vinegar. Marinate as for tarragon vinegar.

Maraschino vinegar
For every 500ml (1 pint) of vinegar you will need 500g (1lb) stoned and crushed maraschino cherries. Marinate for 4 to 5 days in a cool, dark place. Add to lemonade.

Aromatic vinegar
For every litre (2 pints) of ordinary vinegar, take 100g (4oz) tarragon flowers and leaves, celery and dill, black currant leaves, lime flowers and a bay leaf. Marinate as for tarragon vinegar and strain. Use in vegetable salads.

Saffron vinegar
Use only a pinch of saffron to a litre (2 pints) of vinegar. Marinate as for tarragon vinegar. This vinegar has a yellow colour and a pleasant aroma.

Plantago lanceolata

Plates

Sweet Flag

Acorus calamus L.

A perennial plant of the family Araceae, Sweet Flag grows up to 150cm (5ft) high and has a thick, creeping, ringed rootstalk, measuring, on average, 50cm (1ft 8in) long by 3cm (1½in) wide. Its sword-like leaves on triangular stalks grow from rhizomes. The flower-bearing stalk has a reddish base culminating in a greenish-brown spadix of tiny flowers. In temperate climes, Sweet Flag flowers from June to July; it does not bear fruit. It is propagated by rhizome cuttings in damp soil.

Although a native of the swampy areas of the Indian mountain regions, *Acorus calamus* was known to the ancient Greeks and Romans. It was brought to Europe during the Arab invasions and has grown there ever since, abounding in bogs and on the banks of ponds and brooks.

Three kinds of Sweet Flag are available: peeled, unpeeled and candied. Unpeeled Sweet Flag contains most of the essential oil and has the strongest aroma; peeled Sweet Flag is sometimes sold powdered and has a highly aromatic, slightly bitter flavour.

Sweet Flag has been known for its medicinal properties since prehistoric times. The rootstalks are mainly harvested in autumn and, after thorough washing and cleaning, are dried by either natural or artificial means. The dried rootstalks are then used in cooking. Sweet Flag is sometimes added to drinks in the Far East and is also used in the manufacture of beverages. The fresh, bulbous root of Sweet Flag is valued as an emetic, and other medicinal properties include its ability to stimulate digestion and the secretion of gastric juices; it also has carminative properties and is said to alleviate bile disorders.

Common Onion

Allium cepa L.

Shallot

Allium ascalonicum L.

Rocambole

Allium sativum L. ssp. *ophioscorodon* (Link) Holub

The Onion is a plant of the Liliaceae family. Several species are grown in central Europe: the Common Onion is propagated by seed or small bulbs and occurs in many varieties and colours; the Shallot, which is a perennial, propagates vegetatively by auxiliary bulbils; and the Rocambole, which is related to the Leek, produces small, white, glossy bulblets of a delicate taste. Its propagation is vegetative.

The Onion is an edible bulb, native to central Asia and the Mediterranean region, which is today widely cultivated throughout Europe. Shallots, however, originated in Ethiopia and were named after the Palestinian town of Ascalona near which they were cultivated.

Onions are a basic seasoning in the preparation of meat dishes, soups, salads, pickles, sauces, stewed vegetables, pâtés and spreads — they are widely used both in western and oriental cookery. Both the pungent-flavoured bulb of the fresh onion and its young leaves are used, both for eating raw and in cooking; onions are also available in dried or liquid form. Shallots are sharp tasting and are widely used in French, Russian and American cooking, while rocambole, a small delicate onion, is most often used as a garnish, in mixed pickles, and in salad dressings.

Onions contain many biologically valuable substances. They stimulate the liver and pancreas, affect cardiac activity and soothe the nervous system. They help regulate the activity of the pituitary gland and prevent colds. They are extremely wholesome, particularly when eaten raw.

Onions should be grown in light, humus-rich soil and fertilized with compost rather than fresh manure. They can be grown either from 'sets' (smal bulblets) or from seed, and are harvested young, together with the leaves (they are known at this stage as 'spring' or 'green' onions) or when fully ripe and mature when the leaves have begun to wither. Young onions being grown for their leaves can also be grown in winter in pots in a light place.

Welsh Onion (also known as Cibol)

Allium fistulosum L.,
syn. *Allium fistulosum* var. *viviparum* L.

The Welsh Onion forms small, cylindrically elongated bulbs with numerous additional bulblets, so that it looks like a clump. The leaves are a rich green colour and resemble the tubular leaves of the common onion. The height of the plants is 30 to 100 cm (12in to 40in) on average. The Welsh Onion is grown for the leaves which can be eaten all the year round. They have a remarkably high vitamin content, mainly vitamin C; fifteen times higher than that of the Common Onion.

The Welsh Onion is a perennial member of the onion family and is probably indigenous to the Far East, to Siberia and China in particular.

Welsh Onions were unknown in Europe until comparatively recently, while ancient Chinese documents show that it was being cultivated in the Far East more than 2,000 years ago. It is now widely cultivated in both Europe and North America.

As in its original home, the Welsh Onion is grown both for its leaves and for the long, petiolated stem formed by the fleshy bases of the leaves. The stem is very sweet, delicate and extremely tasty. The 'tops' of the variety *A. fistulosum viviparum* can be used in pickles, like Rocambole.

Leek

Allium porrum L.

The Leek belongs to the Liliaceae family and has hollow stalks from 40 to 90cm (16 to 36in) high. Though a biennial, it is usually grown as an annual. The bulb is oblong with a few (or no) sessile bulbils. The leaves are flat, longish and lanceolate, and measure up to 3cm (1in) across. Leek flowers are arranged in rich, large, spherical umbels surrounded by early deciduous leaves and the flower petals are pink.

The Leek, *Allium porrum,* probably derives from *Allium ampeloprasum,* a plant indigenous to the Mediterranean region and the Near East, which has been widely grown for its stem and leaves since ancient times.

While in some parts of Europe the Leek is seen as nothing more than a mere ingredient of soup or stew, the cooks of France have exploited all the delicate qualities of this vegetable. Thus, French haute cuisine boasts in its repertoire recipes for stewed leeks, puréed leeks, leek stuffings and braised leeks. In Czechoslovakia, leeks are served whole, with only the roots and faded leaves being discarded. Throughout the Mediterranean area, the bulblets of the original *A. ampeloprasum* are used as a condiment.

Like other plants of the genus *Allium,* leeks contain essential sulphuric oils as well as the enzyme alliin. Methylalliin and cycloalliin are also present and are responsible for releasing the characteristic leek aroma.

Leeks au Gratin

6 medium leeks
1/8 litre (4fl oz) milk
1/8 litre (4fl oz) cream
3 egg yolks
100g (4oz) grated Gruyère or
   Emmenthal cheese

1 × 15ml spoon (1 tablespoon) mustard
juice of 1/2 lemon
pepper
salt
1 × 15ml spoon (1 tablespoon) butter

Trim the roots and green parts of the leeks. Wash the leeks thoroughly, drain and then cook them for 10 minutes in boiling salted water; drain.
Bring milk and cream to boiling point, remove from the heat and stir in the cheese. Season with mustard, lemon juice, pepper and salt. Arrange the leeks in a greased ovenproof dish. Spoon over the sauce and dot with butter. Cook at 90°C (200°F, Gas Mark 3), for 15 to 20 minutes or until the sauce is well risen and a pale golden colour.

Serves 4

Leek Purée à la Paul Bocuse

500g (1lb) leeks
2 egg yolks
1/16 litre (4 tablespoons) thin
  cream

salt
pinch of nutmeg

Trim the roots and green parts from the leeks. Wash very thoroughly and then drain.
Cut the leeks into thin slices. Add the sliced leeks to a pan and let them stew gently in
their own juices until tender, stirring constantly; do not allow the leeks to colour.
Mix together the egg yolks and cream and add them to the leeks. Season with salt and
nutmeg and cook gently, stirring, until the sauce thickens. Serve with fish, roast meat
or poultry.

Serves 4

Left: *Allium porrum*
Right: *Allium fistulosum*

Chinese Chives

Allium odorum L., syn. *Allium tuberosum*

The Chinese Chive belongs to the Liliaceae family. It forms underground bulbs rather like rhizomes or tubers, hence its synonym *Allium tuberosum*. The Chinese Chive reaches a height of 35 to 45cm (14 to 18in). It has white flowers and is frost-resistant. It can also be propagated easily from seed.

Chinese Chives are a perennial, onion-type vegetable, native to the mountainous regions of China and Mongolia. Cultivation of this plant began in China some 3,000 years ago and it has since become widely popular both for its culinary and medicinal properties.

Chinese Chives have flat leaves unlike their European counterpart *(Allium schoenoprasum)*, and a distinct, very delicate garlic-like odour. Finely chopped leaves are delicious added at the last minute to soups, salads, cottage cheese or meat spreads, to minced meat and pasta dishes, to pies and soufflés.

Gardeners in China usually sow Chinese Chives in mixed beds alongside Chinese Cabbage *(Brassica pekinensis)*, which protects it from pests and diseases. While they are usually grown in the open, more rapid growth can be achieved in hot beds, in greenhouses or under special frames. Chinese Chives can, of course, also be grown in pots on balconies or indoors for harvesting at any season. To harvest them, simply cut them back gradually wih scissors several times during the growing period. In autumn, several clumps may be dug up and brought indoors so that fresh cuttings may be gathered throughout the winter.

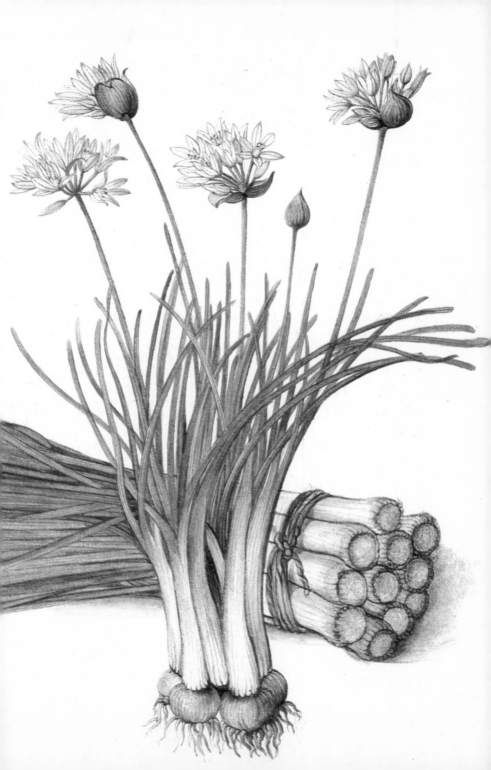

Garlic

Allium sativum L.

This plant belongs to the family Liliaceae. It is a perennial with an underground bulb composed of bulblets, often called *cloves*. The leaves are narrow and flat, green to blue-green in colour. In the varieties with flower axes, the flower stem is terminated by an umbel with several blossoms coated in membranous bracts; it contains 'tops' (bulbils) about 1cm (1/2in) in diameter. Cultivated varieties of Garlic propagate only in the vegetative manner. The tops can be used both for propagation and as a seasoning.

Garlic is one of the oldest vegetables known to man. Originally a native of central Asia, it has now become established throughout the world. It has a pronounced smell and a sharp taste. The fresh cloves are the main source of seasoning, but Garlic is also available in minced, powder or paste form; leaves of the plant may also be used in cookery. Garlic is used throughout the world, particularly in the preparation of meat, fish and vegetable dishes, in sauces, soups and in salads and salad dressings.

Wild Garlic species have a higher content of essential oils and a more pungent taste then the cultivated forms. Garlic contains proteins, glycosides and sugars. One of the components of essential garlic oil is allitin, which is transformed by enzymes into allicin, an efficient bactericide. Sulphur and vitamins B and C are also present. Garlic is said to stimulate secretion of the digestive juices and bile, to soothe the intestinal muscle, to affect the respiratory passages, regulate bacteria in the large intestine, and to increase blood flow in the arteries. It is also said to reduce blood pressure, and is recommended in the treatment of influenza epidemics and for the relief of flatulence.

Chives

Allium schoenoprasum L., syn. *Allium sibiricum* L.

The Chive is a perennial herb of the family Liliaceae. It forms thick clumps of hollow, tubular leaves growing from tiny bulbs. In the second year after sowing, an umbel of pink or purplish flowers appears on the stem. The plant is frost-resistant.

Chives are probably native to the Mediterranean region. In the 16th century they became widely cultivated in central Europe and today grow wild alongside waterways in Europe, North America and Asia. Two species of wild Chives are found in Europe and both resemble the garden varieties, but have smaller, more pungent leaves. *Allium schoenoprasum* is generally found near brooks, while Siberian Chives, *A. sibiricum,* thrive in damp meadows. Both are used in the same way as garden chives. In the wild, they flower from March to May.

Only the fresh young leaves are good as a seasoning; in taste, they are reminiscent of garlic and have a sharp yet sweetish taste. Chives can be used instead of onions in cooked dishes and salads or can be used chopped as a herb (especially in Chinese cooking), in soups and sauces, with vegetables, in spreads and in herb butters.

Chives provide a significant source of vitamin C, carotene, and vitamin B_2. They also contain essential oils with sulphur, a high percentage of sodium, calcium, potassium, phosphorus and iron. They are said to aid the digestion and stimulate the appetite and are considered to be useful for reducing high blood pressure.

Chives may be propagated by seed or by division. They can be grown in beds in the garden or in pots. For fast winter growing, plant divided clumps into pots or boxes in November. Keep them well watered and fertilized in a warm, well-lit position. They are at their best in spring and winter, but can be harvested and used all year round.

Lesser Galangal
(also known as **Siamese Ginger**)

Languas officinarum (Farwell), syn. *Alpinia officinarum* Hance

This plant belongs to the family Zingiberaceae. Its other name is 'Siamese Ginger'. From a perennial, thick, creeping rhizome, the plant sends out stems sometimes surpassing 2m (6ft) in height, and covered by sessile, narrow lanceolate, leathery leaves with membranous ligules and terminated by clusters of greenish-white fragrant flowers. The composition of the inflorescence is similar to that of Ginger. The fruits are pulpous, pea-sized, spherical berries; when mature, they turn red. The berries contain some three rich brown, hard seeds with an unpleasant, bitter taste.

Lesser Galangal resembles Ginger and is thought by some to be superior in taste to it. Its rootstalks are processed into a pungent seasoning, characterized by a spicy smell and tart taste. It is found predominantly in China, Thailand, eastern India and the adjacent islands. It is also cultivated in Japan and in the West Indies. Lesser Galangal is a component of various mixed spices and is sold as a powder, slightly darker in colour than ginger; it may also be bought in dried, brown-red pieces.

As a seasoning, it is best known in the famous Indonesian *nasi goreng* – a dish which originated in south-eastern Asia and which has now become popular in Indonesian restaurants throughout the world, particularly in Holland ('rijstafel'). Lesser Galangal can also be used instead of Ginger in stews, fish dishes, salads, with vegetables and game. In the Middle Ages, this spice was regarded more as a medicament, and it has remained popular in folk medicine to this day. In the 16th century the herbalist Matthioli praised it for the following effects: fragrant breath, good digestion, relief of flatulence and stimulation of carnal desires.

Siamese Chops

4 pork or lamb chops	1 × 5ml spoon (1 teaspoon) galangal
1 × 5ml spoon (1 teaspoon) soy sauce	oil for frying
3 × 15ml spoons (3 tablespoons) to-mato ketchup	2 onions, chopped
	pinch salt
2 × 15ml spoons (2 tablespoons) wine	tomato and cucumber slices for garnish

Bone the chops and cut the meat in 3.5cm (1¹/₂in) pieces. Mix together soy sauce, tomato ketchup, wine and galangal. Add the meat and marinate for about 20 minutes. Fry the onions in the oil for a few minutes. Add the meat and fry gently until tender. Season with salt. Serve with rice and garnish with sliced tomatoes and cucumbers.

Serves 4

Cashew

Anacardium occidentale L.

Cashew, originally known as *Acaju,* is a low-branching tropical tree about 7 to 20m (21 to 60ft) high, with an irregular crown. It belongs to the Anacardiaceae family. The Cashew bears a kidney-shaped nut covered with a thick, horny shell. The stipes of the fruit and the flower disk become swollen during the development of the nut and form a large false fruit in the shape of a short pear. This has a fine skin at full maturation. The pulp is generally a light yellow, with a delicate, refreshing taste.

The Cashew comes from the Amazon river basin and is grown throughout the tropics, especially in India, Mozambique, Tanzania, Ceylon and Brazil.

Cashew nuts have to be roasted before being eaten. They are used in cooking exotic dishes, as well as for eating on their own. The juice from the false fruit can be made into wine, brandy, marmalade and jelly.

The nut is composed of 25 to 30 per cent kernel and 70 to 75 per cent shell. About 35 per cent of the shell consists of a sharp oil called cashew oil, or *cardol,* which has disinfectant properties and is used commercially for a number of different purposes. The false fruit has a high quantity of pectin and about 8 to 15 per cent sugar. It comprises about 75 per cent juice, rich in vitamin C and vitamin B_2. The nuts themselves contain 3.5 to 5 per cent water, 10 to 29 per cent protein, 45 to 61 per cent fat, 8 to 23 per cent nitrogenous extractive substances, some 6 per cent saccharose, 9 to 20 per cent starch and 0.5 to 4 per cent cellulose.

Dill

Anethum graveolens L.

This is an annual plant belonging to the Umbelliferae family. It reaches a height of up to 120cm (4ft), has smooth, pruinose stalks with sessile, palmatisect leaves divided into filiform segments. The yellow flowers are arranged in umbels. The whole plant has the typical dill smell.

Dill is native to the Far East, to Iran and western India. It was brought to northern Europe during the reign of Charles the Great, although in southern Europe it has been cultivated since the 3rd century. The ancient Egyptians used Dill as a medicinal plant and administered it for headaches. Today, it is widely cultivated and used in cooking in America, Asia and, particularly, in northern Europe.

Dill leaves, stalks and seeds are all used as seasonings. The fresh, young dill leaves are best, but dried or preserved Dill can also be used. (Dried Dill should be kept in tightly closed containers.) Dill stalks and unripe seeds are used for pickling vegetables.

Dill goes well with cucumber, both fresh and pickled, in salads, herb butters, spreads, mayonnaise, fish sauces, meat and egg dishes, and cream soups.

The whole Dill plant contains aromatic volatile oils, particularly the seeds (up to 2.5 per cent). Dill is said to stimulate the appetite, and has carminative, slightly diuretic and calming effects.

The cultivation of this plant is extremely simple: it is propagated by seeds sown in April and May in shallow rows 10 to 30cm (4 to 12in) apart — depending on when it is to be harvested. Dill needs frequent watering during the growing period. It can also be grown in boxes or pots in good garden soil. If allowed to ripen it will self-seed freely. The plants should be ready for harvesting within 4 to 6 weeks.

Angelica

Angelica archangelica L.,
syn. *Archangelica officinalis* (Moench/Hoffm.)

This is an annual to perennial herb of the family Umbelliferae, up to 1m (3ft) high, with a hollow, grooved stem, reddish at the base, with a rosette of basal leaves and yellowish or green-white flowers in rich umbels. The fruits are longish, yellowish-coloured diachenes. Angelica is a melliferous plant flowering from July to August.

Angelica grows in northern Asia and Europe, having been brought to central Europe from Scandinavia in the 14th century. In its natural state, in the wild, it is usually found growing high, near brooks and in upper meadowlands.

It is the rhizomes and roots, harvested in the second year of growth, that are the main sources of angelica as used in cooking. All the parts of the plant, however, can be used: stems, flowers, young leaves and fruits. They have a spicy smell and a sharp, bitter taste.

Angelica is a common ingredient used in the manufacture of candies, its fruits and leaves may be added to sauces and salads and sometimes to fruit soups. The main components of Angelica are essential oils, coumarin and furocoumarin derivatives, the bitter principle angelicin, tannins and organic acids. Angelica is said to stimulate the digestion, promote appetite and the secretion of gastric juices; it is also said to regulate peristalsis.

Since the plant increases sensitivity to the sun's rays, great care must be taken during harvesting by those who are susceptible to sun allergies.

The root of the plant is used in the making of liqueurs and vermouth: it is also used as a deodorant and in medicines for its diuretic and digestive properties. In large doses Angelica can be harmful. (It was an important ingredient of medieval 'wonder medicines' taken against poisons.)

Chervil

Anthriscus cerefolium ssp. *sativa* (L.) Hoffman

This annual plant, up to 50cm (20in) high, belongs to the family Umbelliferae. It forms a thickened, tapering root. The fine, multiple-pinnate leaves resemble those of parsley, and the tiny white flowers are arranged in umbels.

Chervil is native to south-eastern Europe and south-western Asia. It was cultivated centuries ago by the ancient Greeks and Romans and by the Middle Ages had become a common European plant. Nowadays, it is mostly cultivated in northern Europe and North America. Wild Chervil is still found in central Europe.

Fresh Chervil leaves, with their agreeable, spicy aniseed-like aroma and slightly sweetish taste, are most frequently used in cooking in the same way as parsley, in salads, dressings, in egg, meat and fish cookery, in herb butters, in sauces and soups and for garnishing canapés. Dried Chervil leaves make a good second best when fresh ones are unavailable.

Chervil contains, among other things, an aromatic essential oil, vitamin C, carotene and minerals such as iron and magnesium. It has slightly diuretic properties, promotes the digestion and is said to relieve flatulence.

Chervil is grown like Parsley (var. *crispum*). It should be sown in early spring in pots and boxes; it is then forced before being planted out in the garden in shallow rows 20cm (8in) apart. Young leaves and stems should be harvested before flowering. For a constant supply of fresh greenery, sow the seeds at fortnightly intervals, plant in loose soil and water frequently.

Celery

Apium graveolens L.,
syn. *Apium graveolens* var. *rapaceum*

Celery is a biennial plant: in the first year, it forms leaves and usually a thickened root, in the second year, flowers and fruits appear. The leaves are pinnate, sometimes with reddish-tinted stalks. The yellowish-white flowers are arranged in umbels. The seed is a small achene.

All Celery varieties are derived from the wild *Apium graveolens* var. *sylvestris* which is indigenous to the marshy, salty soil of the Mediterranean, Asian and African regions. Celery stalks and leaves were used in cooking as far back as in Egyptian times and by the Greeks and Romans. Today, Celery is cultivated throughout the world as a vegetable, seasoning and medicinal plant. Celery leaves can be used as a herb, but should be added sparingly to dishes since they are more pronounced in taste and aroma than, for example, Parsley. Celery is a popular seasoning in Balkan, English, French and American cookery and the stalks, seeds and leaves, either dried or ground, are part of the basic ingredients of many soups, sauces and grilled meat recipes.

Celery leaves are rich in vitamin C, carotene, proteins, minerals – particularly phosphorus and iron – essential oil, vegetal hormones and glycosides (apiin). Celery root comprises purines, essential oils, proteins, glycides, apiin, cholin, vitamins B_1, B_2, PP and C, minerals (calcium, sodium, magnesium, potassium and phosphorus).

Horseradish

Armoracią rusticana Lam. G. M. and Sch.

Horseradish is a perennial plant of the family Cruciferae. It has a long, thick and fleshy root out of which grow leafy stems. The large basal leaves have long petioles and roughly crenate, oblong blades. It flowers from May to July; the white flowers are arranged in racemes. The fruits are siliquas, which rarely ripen in central Europe.

While Horseradish is native to southeastern Europe it has been cultivated in central Europe since the 12th century — and now even grows wild in this region.

For culinary purposes, Horseradish is best used fresh — traditionally it should be grated, mixed with seasonings and cream and served with rare roast beef; it can also be grated and added to pickled vegetables, to sauces for fish and meat, or to eggs and cheese.

Horseradish contains vitamin C, potassium, calcium, magnesium and iron, the glycoside sinigrine, mustard oil, the myrozine enzyme and phytoncides. It is said to have several medicinal qualities: for example, to stimulate gastro-intestinal activity, to dissolve phlegm, and to act as a diuretic. It should be consumed in early spring to supply the body with vitamin C, lacking after a long winter. Because of its digestive attributes, it is recommended as a relish to be served with fatty or indigestible meals.

Horseradish can be propagated annually from cuttings taken in autumn. These should be placed in sand boxes in a cool, dark room. In March, the seedlings should be planted out in beds of light, sandy soil in horizontal rows about 8cm (3in) deep and 18cm (7in) apart. The cuttings will be free of buds apart from about 2cm (1in) at each end. The straight, thick roots should be ready for easy harvesting in October. Simply cut off the lateral roots and start again, using them for harvesting the following year.

Southernwood (also known as **Lad's Love**)

Artemisia abrotanum L

Southernwood is probably indigenous to western Asia and has for centuries been popular for its pleasant, lemon-like smell and favourable medicinal effects. This is a densely branched semi-shrub, a perennial herb of the Compositae family. The leaves are smooth on the surface and hairy beneath. The whole plant has a spicy, lemony fragrance. The flowers are pale yellow and the fruit is a small, brownish achene. In central and northern Europe it flowers less frequently than in Asia and occasionally does not even bear fruit.

Both fresh and dried leaves are used in cooking as herbs and in the commercial preparation of liqueurs and mixed alcoholic drinks. They can also be added to game sauces, stewed vegetables, salads, mayonnaises, stewed meats and vegetables. Southernwood has a slightly bitter tang and should only be used sparingly for flavouring; always keep it in the dark in a tightly covered container.

Southernwood contains essential oils, tannins, bitter principles, abrotamin and other, as yet uninvestigated, substances. It is said to promote the appetite and good digestion, and reputedly has calming effects.

It grows well in light, dry soil, rich in humus. In central Europe, where it does not produce seeds, it is propagated by division and will grow for years if planted in the right spot. In autumn, and again in spring, the old stems should be cut back to rejuvenate the growing shrub which will then produce thriving new shoots.

Common Wormwood

Artemisia absinthium L.

Common Wormwood is a perennial herb of the family Compositae. From the branched rhizome grows at first a rosette of basal, long-petioled, palmate leaves with narrow lanceolate segments, and later an up to 100cm (40in) high stem with a woody base. The whole plant is covered with silver-grey fibrous hairs. The tiny, tubular yellow flowers arranged in heads open from June to August. The fruit is a small, brown striped achene.

Common Wormwood is native to Asia, Africa, central and southern Europe and the temperate zone of America. It was used by the ancient Egyptians both for medicinal and culinary purposes and later in ancient Greece and Rome. Today, it grows wild on railway embankments, road verges, warm rocky slopes and limestone areas; sometimes it turns up in fields and gardens.

Only the young leaves or non-woody tops of Wormwood are used in cooking. They should be collected in dry weather, shortly before flowering and are used, fresh or dry, in very small quantities.

With its highly aromatic, slightly bitter taste, Wormwood is valued as one of the special ingredients that go into vermouth and bitter digestive cordials; it is also used to aromatize cognac and other spirits (absinthe is the best example of these). For cooking purposes, only very small quantities need be used for flavouring because of its intensely tart taste and strong smell. Wormwood may be added to boiled pork dishes, as a seasoning for roast mutton, goose or duck, or it can be added to batter for pancakes.

Wormwood contains mainly essential oils (especially thujone and azulene), glycosidic bitter principles and phytoncides. It is said to stimulate secretion of the gastric juices and the appetite, and to activate the bile; it acts as a disinfectant and anthelmintic. Prolonged use of Wormwood, either as a medicine or a herb, should be avoided: excessive use increases blood circulation in the mucous membrane of the stomach and provokes vertigo. It should not be taken during pregnancy.

Tarragon

Artemisia dracunculus L.

A perennial, densely branched plant of the family Compositae, Tarragon reaches a height of up to 100cm (40in). It grows shoots from underground rhizomes. The leaves are linear, lanceolate, smooth and green, 3 to 6cm (1 ¼ to 2 ½in) long, with entire margins. Tarragon flowers from August to October in heads of tiny white to pinkish flowers with yellow scales. The whole plant has an aromatic odour.

Tarragon is indigenous to the south-eastern region of the USSR and central Asia and is today cultivated mainly in Europe, Asia and America. Two accepted culinary types of Tarragon exist — French and Russian. Tarragon is prized by cooks worldwide, while another variety, Russian Tarragon, *(A. dracunculoides)* has an unpleasant flavour and should be avoided.

Only the leaves, preferably fresh, are used in cooking. Tarragon is used throughout the world in cookery but occupies a special place in French and Armenian cuisines; it is also used abundantly in the United States. Tarragon is ideal for flavouring vinegars, herb butters, soups, stews, and has a special affinity with fish and poultry; it is also used in salads, mustards and marinades.

Tarragon contains essential oil, enzymes, tannins and bitter principles; fresh Tarragon also contains vitamins, has a high percentage of minerals and a high iodine content. It has a mild diuretic effect and is said to have antisclerotic properties; it is an excellent flavouring for salt-free diets.

Tarragon thrives in sunny spots, in well-fertilized soil. It can only be propagated by division. The leaves should be harvested just before flowering, either in spring or autumn, and the stems should be cut back to within 10cm (4in) of the ground to rejuvenate the plant.

Mugwort

Artemisia vulgaris L.

Mugwort is a perennial herb of the Compositae family. The multiple rhizome sends out stiff-branched stems reaching 150cm (30in) in height. These are thick and grooved, and russet to purple in colour. The leaves are pinnate and lyre-shaped – dark green and smooth above, off-white and felted below. On the upper part of the stem, the leaves become lanceolate with entire margins. The small, tawny to reddish many-rayed flowers are arranged in dense, leafy panicles. They appear from late July onwards. The fruits are flat achenes.

Mugwort grows wild in Europe, Asia and northern Africa, both in lowland and upland regions. A member of the genus *Artemisia,* it is less in need of a warm climate than Common Wormwood, thriving in abundance on the roadside, and indeed in warm countries it tends to become a persistent weed. Since the time of the Celts, it has been valued for its so-called magical properties and its ability to ward off evil spirits and disease.

As a herb in cooking, the young leaves or flowers of Mugwort can be used in either fresh or dried form; it is also used for medicinal purposes. While still aromatic, Mugwort is less bitter than Common Wormwood.

Since Mugwort grows in abundance in the wild, it is not grown domestically. The young leaves and plant tops should be harvested from July to September from plants just in flower; cuttings should be allowed to dry naturally.

Mugwort contains an essential oil in its stalks and leaves (with thujone and cineol), bitter principles, inulin, cholin and terpenes. It is beneficial for the digestion and the secretion of gastric juices; it promotes the appetite, acts as a carminative and calms spasms of the intestinal tract.

It is used both as a seasoning and a medicinal plant. It is added to slightly bitter alcoholic drinks. Young stems and leaves in a small quantity (1 teaspoon to 2 litres [4 pints]) may be used to flavour vegetable soups, game sauces, minced meat dishes, and minced stuffings. Dried panicles add zest to roast goose or duck (crushed panicles are used as stuffing), or to fat pork or roast mutton. In a small quantity, fresh Mugwort can be used to season salads. It also aromatizes pancake batter.

Borage

Borago officinalis L.

Borage is an annual plant of the family Boraginaceae, reaching a height of 30 to 46cm (12 to 18in), with branched stems and opposite, wrinkled leaves up to 10cm (4in) long. The whole plant is covered with tough bristles. It has bright blue or white, five-lobed flowers, which appear from June to September. It is an ornamental and melliferous plant.

Borage is native to southern Europe, where it still grows wild, but in its cultivated form it has spread northwards into central Europe.

Only the fresh young leaves are used in cooking. With its cucumber-like taste and smell Borage is best served with cucumber, tomato and potato salads, with vegetable and meat stews, in mayonnaise, with cheese spreads, fish dishes and grilled meat. The young leaves, and sometimes the pretty blue flowers, too, can be used as a garnish for summer drinks.

Borage is also a medicinal plant, containing mainly mucilages (up to 30 per cent), resins, saponins, asparagin, silicic acid, tannins, antocyanic pigment and essential oils. Fresh Borage also contains vitamins; of its mineral content, manganese is the most important. Borage has diuretic and slightly laxative properties, and has anti-inflammatory effects. It is said to strengthen the nervous system. An English saying, derived from Pliny, maintains that 'Borage gives courage'. Freshly pressed juice of the plant is believed to reduce spring fatigue, by accelerating the metabolism and thus acting as a general pick-me-up.

Borage can be grown in gardens, in boxes or in pots. Seeds should be sown in shallow rows in early April. If raising Borage indoors or under glass, the seedlings will sprout within a week. They can be grown as early as February under these protected conditions.

Herb Butter

150g (5oz) butter
1 × 15ml spoon (1 tablespoon) finely chopped borage
1 × 15ml spoon (1 tablespoon) finely chopped dill
1 × 15ml spoon (1 tablespoon) finely chopped parsley
squeeze of lemon juice
1 × 5ml spoon (1 teaspoon) chopped onion
pinch salt
pinch pepper

Blend together all the ingredients. Spread the mixture on canapés or grilled meat.

White Mustard

Sinapis alba L.

Black Mustard

Brassica nigra (L.) Koch

Indian Mustard

Brassica juncea (L.) Czern.

The three species are closely related and look alike. They are all annual plants of the Cruciferae family. White and Black Mustard grow in the Mediterranean region while Indian Mustard grows in the Far East.

The seeds of all three species, red-brown, pale yellow, and pale brown respectively, are used as a seasoning and processed into the mustard powder (dry mustard) which is so popular (sometimes mixed with cayenne pepper) in Britain and the USA. Semi-liquid cooking mustard is made from the mustard flour which remains after the oil has been pressed. This is blended with vinegar, salt, sugar and various spices before artificial dyes and preservatives are added.

Culinary mustard is not simply a condiment, but an essential ingredient of salad dressings, mayonnaise, meat dishes and pickles. Whole mustard seeds may be added to preserved vegetables and to fish; ground mustard seeds are sometimes used in mixtures for spiced wines and vermouth.

Mustard contains the glycoside sinigrin and sinalbin, decomposing into pungent essential mustard oil and proteins.

Mustard is not at all difficult to grow – any soil or climate will do. The seeds are sown in rows in spring.

Roast Rabbit with Mustard

1 whole rabbit, skinned, paunched and trussed
salt
pepper
225g (8oz) unsmoked streaky bacon

3 × 15ml spoons (3 tablespoons) French mustard
1 × 5ml spoon dried tarragon
1 glass dry white wine

Sprinkle the rabbit with salt, pepper and tarragon. Cover one side of each bacon slice with mustard and place, mustard side down, on the rabbit. Put the rabbit in a meat tin and roast it in a moderate oven until tender. Remove the bacon slices and arrange the rabbit on a warmed serving dish. Keep the rabbit hot. Strain the juices in the tin into a clean pan and add the wine. Check the seasoning and add salt and pepper, if necessary. Reheat the sauce and serve with the rabbit.

Serves 4

White Cinnamon (also known as Canella)

Canella alba Murray

Persea caryophyllata Martius,
syn. *Dicypellium caryophyllatum* (Martius) Nees

White Cinnamon belongs to the family Canelaceae (Winteraceae). It grows wild in the Antilles, Florida and mostly in the Bahamas. It yields an aromatic bark which is orange-yellow on the surface. The inner surface is off-white, hard and brittle, with a sharp, spicy taste, reminiscent of clove and nutmeg.

Pieces of the bark, with the outer cork removed, are used as a seasoning or medicament. It is popularly used as an aromatic addition to liqueurs.

The bark of the White Cinnamon, sometimes also known as *winterana,* is used as a substitute for winter's bark *(Crotex coto)* — a well known medicine for yellow fever and stomach problems. True winter's bark is obtained from the tree *Drimys winteri.*

A similar tree, *Persea caryophyllacea,* grows in tropical America, mainly in Brazil. The dried bark, which is very similar, contains an essential oil, resins and tannins and is used to make medicine.

Caper

Capparis spinosa L.

The Caper is a low, trailing shrub with slender, trailing stalks. It grows wild or cultivated in the Mediterranean region. The shrub is generally 1 to 1.5m (3 to 4½ft) high. The leaves are petiolate, ovate, and the tiny stipules underneath the petioles are modified into short thorns. It flowers in July and August. The large white or pale pink flowers grow individually, on long stalks, from leaf axils. Each flower has four petals, four sepals, and many stamens with mauve filaments. The fruit is an oblong or pear shaped, multi-seeded capsule.

Several decades ago, when Capers were less valued as a condiment, they were replaced by buds of other plants, such as Broom, Buttercup, Nasturtium or Ficaria. Good quality Capers are firm and closed, olive green in colour, turning a slightly mottled red at the tip. Capers contain the volatile glycoside, rutin.

Matthioli, the medieval herbalist, recommended that Capers pickled in vinegar and salt be 'taken before meals, since they promote the appetite and open the liver'. There may be some truth in this maxim, since Capers are usually served as part of hors d'oeuvres.

The closed flower buds are used, pickled in vinegar, salt or wine, in cooking. They have a piquant, slightly bitter taste and improve the flavour of sauces for fish in particular. Capers are also used to add spice to salads, mayonnaise, and as a garnish for cold appetizers.

Cod à la Terst

1kg (2lb) cod cutlets
salt
pepper
2 × 15ml spoons (2 tablespoons) olive
  oil
1 × 15ml spoon (1 tablespoon) capers

6 olives
7 × 15ml spoons (7 tablespoons) dry
  white wine
1 × 15ml spoon (1 tablespoon) lemon
  juice

Sprinkle the cod with salt and pepper. Heat the oil in a pan and fry the fish quickly until golden brown on both sides. Add the remaining ingredients, reduce the heat, cover and simmer for 20 minutes or until the fish is cooked. Serve with boiled potatoes and a green salad.

Serves 4

Pepper

Capsicum annuum L.

This pepper species is probably native to South America, from where it has spread into warm areas all over the world. The fruit is either a pendant or erect, usually conical berry, of various sizes, and may be up to 12cm (5in) long and 4cm (1¾in) wide at the base. The ripe berries may be of various colours but are usually red.

The genus *Capsicum* embodies more than 100 species and classification of this genus is far from unified. The fruits have various names: red pepper, paprika, cayenne pepper, chilli pepper, sweet pepper, Indian pepper, Spanish pepper and so on. Most experts agree, however, that there are two cultivated species: *Capsicum annuum* and *Capsicum frutescens*. Both species have numerous varieties, cultivars and forms and both are used all over the world as vegetables, medicaments and seasonings.

Peppers are divided into sweet-fruited vegetables, often eaten in a green, unripe form, and spice peppers, which are harvested after they have ripened and are used as a condiment. They may be sweet, mild or hot; the pungency is caused by an alkaloid substance called capsicin found in the skin cells, seeds and partitions of the berries.

Ground pepper is used as a common condiment (e.g. paprika) in cooking, in the production of smoked meats, sausages, and cheeses, in ketchups and marinades.

Pepper contains sugars, proteins, capsicin, pigments, fats, essential oils, vitamins C, A, B and nicotinic acid in varying proportions, according to the species.

Beef à l'Esterhazy

750g (1½lb) rump steak
1 × 15ml spoon (1 tablespoon) lard or
  dripping
salt
pepper
1 × 15ml spoon (1 tablespoon) paprika
pinch chilli powder
2 onions, chopped
2 green peppers, chopped

1 × 15ml spoon (1 tablespoon) flour
250ml (8fl oz) beef stock
1 × 15ml (1 tablespoon) chopped parsley
7 × 15ml spoons (7 tablespoons)
  Tokay wine
1 × 15ml spoon (1 tablespoon) lemon
  juice
120ml (4fl oz) soured cream

Cut the steak into 3.75cm (1½in) pieces. Heat the lard in a pan, add the steak and brown quickly on all sides, then remove from the pan. Season with salt, pepper, paprika and chilli powder. Add the onions and peppers and cook gently for 5 minutes.

Blend in the flour, cook for 2 minutes and then return the steak to the pan with the stock and parsley. Cover and simmer for 15 minutes or until the steak is tender. Blend in the wine and lemon juice. Simmer for 2 minutes, stirring all the time. Add the soured cream and reheat but do not boil.

Serves 4

Red Pepper
(also known as **Bell Pepper** or **Pimiento**)
Capsicum annuum L. ssp. *microcarpum*

All the pepper species belong to the Solanaceae family.

The Red Pepper is no longer considered to be an exotic spice or vegetable and, from its home in tropical South America, it has become naturalized in the temperate areas of the world. It exists in mild and pungent varieties and is eaten accordingly, as a vegetable or as a condiment. The ripe, red berries of the fleshy, long-fruited varieties are ground to powder to produce paprika. Other cultivars bear large, short-fruited square berries wih rounded edges. These peppers are eaten as a vegetable, either raw, stewed, baked or pickled. Pungency, in various degrees, is the common denominator: the hot varieties are popular in southern Europe: Bulgaria, Hungary, Italy and Spain, in particular.

Kimtchi Salad
(Korea)

1kg (2lb) Chinese leaves or white cabbage, finely shredded
250g (9oz) white radish, peeled and cut in thin strips
1 onion, sliced

2 garlic cloves, crushed
50g (2oz) chilli pepper, chopped
3 × 15ml spoons (3 tablespoons) salt
1 × 15ml (1 tablespoon) vinegar

Mix together all the ingredients and place them in a large earthenware pot. Press down firmly, cover with a large plate and place a heavy weight on the plate. Allow to stand in a cool place for several days.

Serves 4 to 6

'Roqueto' Pepper

Capsicum baccatum L., syn. *C. pendulum* Willdenow

The 'Roqueto' Pepper from Peru is a perennial, sparsely but widely branched shrub with individual flowers which have purple corolla lobes. The leaves are grey-green and covered with soft hairs. The fruits, which are relatively large with a thick pulp, are smooth and turn purple when mature. They are spherical towards the calyx, becoming slightly conical and ending in a pointed protuberance.

'Roqueto' is grown in the tropical regions of Central and South America. (It is unknown in Europe.) Its seeds are black and wrinkled, unlike other pepper species and its flesh is extremely hot. 'Roqueto' is an essential ingredient of traditional dishes such as Tamales and Chilli con Carne; fiery hot Tabasco sauce is made from the macerated pulp of this pepper.

Internally administered, the extract of 'Roqueto' acts as a powerful stimulant which regulates digestion; it may also be applied externally to relieve rheumatism.

'Roqueto' is unsuitable for drying because of its relatively thick, soft flesh, but it provides first-rate material for purées, sauces, pastes and hot extracts.

Picadillo

1kg (2lb) chuck steak
1/2 litre (3/4 pint) stock or water
black pepper, salt
4 × 15ml spoons (4 tablespoons) olive, vegetable or salad oil
3 garlic cloves, chopped
2 onions, chopped
4 green peppers, de-seeded and chopped
750g (1½lb) tomatoes, skinned, de-seeded and chopped
1 × 15ml spoon (1 tablespoon) de-seeded and chopped chilli pepper
pinch of ground cloves or allspice
3 × 5ml spoons (3 teaspoons) salt
2 × 15ml spoons (2 tablespoons) olives
50g (2oz) raisins
2 × 15ml spoons (2 tablespoons) vinegar
6 eggs

Cut the steak into 3.75cm (1½in) pieces and season with salt and pepper. Put the pieces of steak in a pan, cover with water or stock and simmer for one hour or until the beef is tender.

Heat the oil in another pan, add the garlic, onions, green peppers, chilli pepper and tomatoes and fry gently for 5 minutes. Add the cloves, salt and pepper and cook together gently until the sauce thickens.

Add the olives, raisins and vinegar and simmer for about 5 minutes. Add the cooked beef pieces 2 minutes before serving time.

In a frying pan, fry one egg per person and top each serving with a fried egg.

Serves 6

Cayenne Pepper

Capsicum frutescens L.

Cayenne Pepper is a perennial plant often cultivated as an annual. This species is grown mainly in the tropics; it is often left in the field for 3 to 4 years, although the produce sharply declines after the first productive season. The plant reaches 60cm (24in) in height on average, but some varieties, especially in dry parts of Africa, are smaller.

The fruits of this pepper are deep red and extremely pungent; they are usually sold under the catchall name of chillies; dried, ground chillies are called cayenne pepper.

The discovery of prehistoric remains of this pepper in ancient burial grounds in Peru has established that this species was well distributed throughout the New World long before the 'discovery' of America by Columbus. It was the Spanish and Portuguese in their persistent search for spices who welcomed this new, much more pungent American pepper and popularized it.

Chillies contain quantities of vitamin C, A and E.

Chilli con Carne
(Mexico)

500g (1lb) chuck steak
500g (1lb) pork
100g (4oz) ham
125g (5oz) fat
pinch of caraway seed
25g (1oz) chilli peppers, de-seeded and chopped
2 garlic cloves, crushed
pinch of dried oregano
200g (8oz) red kidney beans, soaked overnight

200g (8oz) haricot beans, soaked overnight
250ml (8fl oz) stock
2 large onions, sliced
500g (1lb) tomatoes, skinned, de-seeded and chopped
2 green peppers, de-seeded and thinly sliced

Cut all the meat into 3.75cm (1½in) pieces. Heat half the fat in a pan and brown the meat quickly on all sides. Add the caraway seeds, chilli pepper, garlic and oregano. Add the beans and stock, cover and simmer gently until meat and beans are tender, about 3 hours.

Heat the remaining fat in another pan and add the onions, tomatoes and peppers. Cover and simmer very gently for about 30 minutes. Add the vegetables to the meat and beans about 10 minutes before the end of cooking time.

Serves 8—10

Papaya (also known as **Melon Tree**)
Carica papaya L.

This is a tropical, perennial plant reaching a height of up to 10m (30ft), and the average diameter of the trunk is about 30cm (12in). It is reminiscent of a palm: it usually has an unbranched cylindrical trunk terminated by a crown of long-petiolate leaves. The trunk is greyish-brown and hollow in older specimens, bearing numerous scars left by fallen leaves. The fruit is oblong, resembling a melon and is usually yellowish-green, yellow, or orange. It can be very large, as much as 10 to 30cm (4 to 12in) long. The fruit is hollow and the surface of the inner wall is covered by many blackish, wrinkled seeds wrapped in a juicy, sour-sweet coating. The seeds have a pungent, peppery taste. The pulp may be as much as 5cm (2in) thick, orange, yellow to orange-red. The whole plant is lactiferous, yielding, when tapped, a white latex, containing the proteclytic enzyme papain.

The fruits of the Papaya are mainly eaten fresh as a dessert or in fruit salads, and are used in the manufacture of soft drinks, ice creams, jams, and stewed fruit. Papaya can also be candied.

Papaya contains 85 to 88 per cent water and 12 to 15 per cent dry matter, including 8 to 12 per cent sugar. The fruits are also rich in vitamins C and A.

Papaya yields the digestive enzyme papain, which has similar effects to pepsin and trypsin. This enzyme comes from the dry latex of the Papaya fruits: the unripe fruits are gently cut open and the dripping latex is stored and then dried, either in the sun or by artificial means. The resulting papain is used throughout the world in medicine and in brewing and the food industry (where it is used as a meat tenderizer).

Caraway

Carum carvi L.

Caraway is a biennial, sometimes perennial, herbaceous plant of the carrot family (Umbelliferae), growing up to 25 to 60cm (10 to 24in) in height. Leaves are double or triple-pinnate, flowers are white, small, and in compound umbels. Ripe fruits divide into two independent achenes.

Caraway is one of the oldest spices known to man: remains have been found dating from the Neolithic era. In those days, it was used in cooking and particularly in medicine and as a magic plant to chase off evil spirits. Today, it grows wild in meadows and pastures throughout central and northern Europe, in some Asian regions and in Canada.

Pale to dark brown in colour, caraway seeds have a distinctive aroma and pungent taste. Young leaves, which have a similar aroma and contain vitamins, enzymes, organic acids and other substances, can also be used in cooking.

Caraway seeds are used in the manufacture of liqueurs (Kümmel is the best-known example), in rye bread, rolls and biscuits, in mixed spices, in vegetable and meat dishes and with roast goose and duck. Fresh Caraway leaves can also be added to soups, salads and cheese spreads. The seeds should be stored in the dark, in tightly closed jars; they should be ground before use.

Caraway seeds contain between 3 and 6.5 per cent essential oils; their main components are carvone (50 to 70 per cent) and the terpene limonene. Caraway also contains proteins, sugar and pentosans. The seeds are said to stimulate the function of the stomach, soothe gastric activity and prevent flatulence and intestinal spasms. It is also believed to stimulate the appetite. The seeds should be picked early in the morning in June.

Wormseed

Chenopodium ambrosioides L.

Wormseed is an annual plant of the family Chenopodiaceae. The erect stems are about 30 to 50cm (12 to 20in) high, with elongated, toothed bottom leaves. The upper leaves are lanceolate, with smooth edges. The flowers are small and greenish-yellow. Both leaves and flowers are covered with scent glands.

Wormseed comes from South America and Mexico where it is used as a medicinal plant and condiment by the Indians. It is cultivated in Europe and North America as well.

For seasoning purposes, either the crushed dried tops are used (collected during flowering) or the leaves and blossoms are used separately. Wormseed has a pleasant, spicy, camphor-like smell and a sharp taste.

As a seasoning it is used in the maximum dose of 1.5ml spoonful (1 teaspoonful) of crushed, dried wormseed to 1 kg (2.2lb) of food. It is added to stewed meat and vegetables, and is also used for flavouring liqueurs.

Wormseed contains an aromatic essential oil (with the constituent askaridol), bitter principles, tannins, resins, saponins, organic acids and other substances. Like many herbs it is poisonous in large quantities, but harmless as a seasoning. It is often prescribed as an anti-spasmodic, to promote appetite and as an expectorant. It also has calming effects and it is an important anthelmintic agent. It is used in perfumery as well.

Wormseed does well in loamy garden soil, in warm, sheltered places. Since it is susceptible to spring frosts, it is better to pre-plant it in boxes and prick out the seedlings in mid-May. Wormseed is harvested in the flowering stage and, although the whole shoot can be used, the leaves and flowers alone give better results. Drying is done in the shade at temperatures not exceeding 35°C (95°F). The plants need to be carefully turned during drying.

Cassia Bark Tree

Cinnamomum cassia Blume

The Cassia Bark Tree resembles the Cinnamon to which it is closely related. It has a heavier appearance, and its bark is cracked, ash-grey, thicker and rougher. The leaves are larger, narrower and longer. Cassia is less fragrant than cinnamon and sometimes has an astringent taste.

Cassia is cultivated mainly in southern China, eastern India and Indonesia.

The small, underdeveloped fruits of the Cassia Bark Tree are collected and sold as 'cassia buds'. They are used in the manufacture of liqueurs and chocolate. They contain one to three per cent essential oil and have a pleasant smell.

Cassia is more easily cultivated than Cinnamon. It is grown mostly from seed. However, the roots are very delicate and must never be damaged or totally uncovered during transplanting.

Cinnamon

Cinnamomum zeylanicum Blume

Cinnamon is an evergreen tropical tree of the family Lauraceae. It reaches a height of 6 to 10m (18 to 30ft). The foliage is pale green with a pronounced venation and the leaves and small flowers form loose panicular inflorescences with a distinctive, pleasant smell. The bark is grey-brown to yellow-grey and smooth.

Cinnamon is native to tropical Asia, and cinnamon bark has been used there as a seasoning for centuries. It was also used in ancient Egypt as a medicament and for flavouring drinks.

Cinnamon bark, which is used for seasoning, is cut from the young shoots of the tree twice a year, in May and October. The bark is peeled off the twigs, tied into faggots and left to ferment under matting for a couple of days. The outer layer of cork and the inner pithy part is removed and the cleaned bark is then left to dry in the sun. This produces the yellow-brown cinnamon we know as a seasoning. The bark scrolls are graded according to colour, thickness and size. Cinnamon is generally used to flavour pastry, cakes and drinks. It is also used in perfumery.

Cinnamon yields an essential oil, both from the bark and the leaves, twigs and roots. It contains the substance eugenol and the aldehyde, cinnamol.

Cinnamon is cultivated in plantations in the form of small shrubs, since the best bark comes from young trees. The shrubs are usually grown from seed and then transplanted. Cinnamon flourishes in a hot, moist environment.

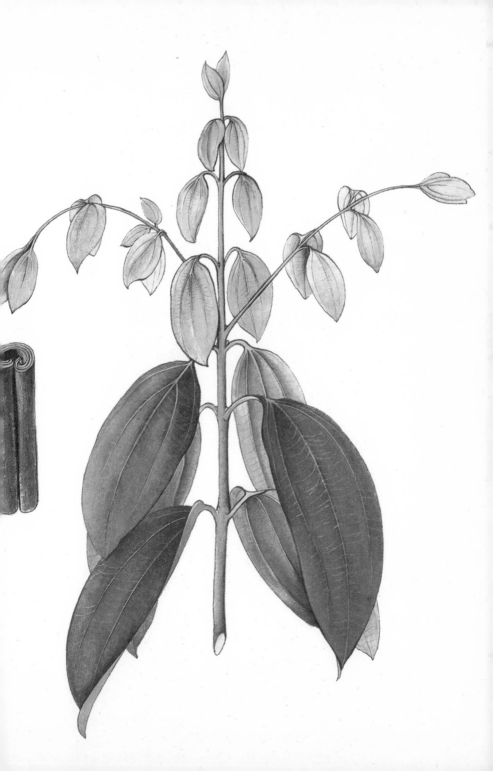

Seville Orange (also known as **Sour Orange**)

Citrus aurantium L.

This sub-tropical tree can grow up to 10m (30ft) high. It has a compact, spherical crown with thorny branches. The young shoots and leaves are pale green. The leaves are elliptically ovate, with a strong smell when crushed. The petioles are widely flattened. The blossoms are large and fragrant, sometimes with double flowers. The fruits are about the same size as a medium-sized orange. The rind is bright orange to reddish, and is thick, bitter and very aromatic. The pulp is composed of 10 to 12 segments and is dark yellow to orange with a sour, bitter taste. The Seville Orange closely resembles the Sweet Orange *(Citrus sinensis)*.

The Seville Orange is native to India, from where it spread to Europe before its cousin, the Sweet Orange. It has also spread to the West Indies and the Near East, as well as to North Africa. The Arabs discovered the Seville Orange at the end of the 9th century and brought it to the Iberian peninsula during the Moorish invasion − the town of Seville presumably gave the orange its name.

The fruit is principally used for making a very rich marmalade and the flowers, the young shoots and the unripe fruits yield a fragrant essential oil much used in the perfumery trade. The unripe fruits are also used to make bitter digestive liqueurs. A similar species, Bergamot *(Citrus aurantium* ssp. *bergamia),* is used for flavouring drinks, as the essential oil contained in the rind is very aromatic.

Lemon

Citrus limon (L.) Burm

The Lemon tree grows mostly in the sub-tropics and is a low, evergreen tree with a rounded or extended irregular crown. Its branches are thick and usually very thorny with pale, oval leaves and short, segmented petioles. The flowers, pink on the outside and creamy-white inside, give off a pleasant scent. Lemons, the fruit of the Lemon tree, are berries which narrow at each end into conical points. Lemon rind is strong, either smooth or rough, ranging in colour from pale green to yellow, with a pleasant, fresh scent. Composed of segments, the pulp is sour and juicy.

Lemon trees were originally grown in south-eastern India, from where the cultivation extended both westward and to the north-east. The Arabs were the first westerners to cultivate Lemons and they introduced the Lemon into the Mediterranean region. Around 1655, the first street vendors selling lemonade appeared in Paris. Since the 17th century, the cultivation of Lemon trees has spread in most sub-tropical zones.

Both the lemon rind and the juice are used in cooking – in pastries, sauces, pâtés and puddings. It is used to flavour drinks and is used extensively by confectioners and liqueur makers. It makes a good substitute for vinegar in salad dressings.

Inferior lemons are processed to provide citric acid and the yellow rind yields the essential citric oil. Lemons have a high content of vitamins (they were used in the Middle Ages to cure scurvy).

Citron

Citrus medica L.

This is a sub-tropical, low tree or shrub with an irregular crown. Its leaves are elliptical with narrow petioles and the large flowers are white inside and purple on the outside. The fruit is elliptically oblong, 6 to 20cm (3 to 8in) long and 5 to 10cm (2 to 4in) thick. Citron berries are quite large and fragrant with a green-yellow to golden-yellow thick rind which may be rough or smooth. The pulp, containing several seeds, can be yellowish-white or green and is aromatic and sour.

The Citron tree is probably indigenous to the valleys of the eastern Himalayas, and may also be native to Cambodia and Yunnan, a province of China. It has been grown for centuries in many varieties. As far back as 300 BC the Citron tree was cultivated by the Medes and Persians, and the Greeks came to know it as the 'Median apple'. The Greeks also used the fruit of the Citron tree to make a famous snake-bite antidote. The Romans used the Citron tree as an ornamental shrub and these trees decorated the gardens and *atria* of rich Romans.

The Citron tree is now cultivated widely in the western Mediterranean and in the Azores. The rind and pulp are removed and the fruit soaked, blanched and dried to provide a citric extract which is added to pastry or used as a filling in confectionery. It makes a delicate flavouring agent, widely used in bakeries.

Clitocybe odora (Fries) Kummer

The cap of *Clitocybe odora* is conical when young and becomes funnel-shaped later. Its edges are wavy and the surface smooth. The short cylindrical stalk is sturdy and supple, becoming soft and mushy or hollow with age. The young mushrooms have a conspicuous copper-green to blue-green, green-grey to whitish colour. The gills are thin, and rather paler than the cap. The flesh of the cap is pale green and smells strongly of aniseed.

This mushroom grows in fallen leaves in deciduous and coniferous (particularly spruce) forests from August to November. It has a delicate, slightly bitter-sweet taste which is strong enough to preclude its use in cooking in large quantities. It can be used fresh or dry.

Creamy Mushroom Sauce

50g (2oz) bacon
15ml (1tablespoon) oil
1 onion, chopped
300g (11oz) mixed mushrooms
    (field mushrooms, *Boletus*
    badius or puffballs), chopped
a few caps *Clitocybe odora,* chopped

1/2 stock cube
pinch curry powder
pinch black pepper
salt
75ml (5 tablespoons) double cream
lemon juice
15ml (1 tablespoon) chopped parsley

Chop the bacon and fry gently in oil for a few minutes until slightly browned. Add the onion and fry until softened. Add the mushrooms, stock cube and seasonings and cook slowly until the mushrooms are tender. Stir in the cream, season to taste, adding a squeeze of lemon, if you like, and sprinkle with parsley. Serve hot or cold with grilled or boiled meat, fish or hard-boiled eggs.

Coco Palm

Cocos nucifera L.

The Coco Palm belongs to the group Ceroxylinae, of the family Arecaceae. It is an unbranched tree, about 5 to 30m (15 to 90ft) high with a pillar-like, curved trunk. The fallen leaf petioles leave conspicuous scars on the trunk. Coco Palms are found in the tropics, near the sea. Their place of origin is not known.

The Coco Palm has a variety of uses. The fruit of the Coco Palm, coconuts, are used to provide both fabric (matting, carpet and ropes) and food. The main product from the Coco Palm is copra — the dried fruit kernels. These yield a colourless to pale yellow-brown oil which solidifies into a whitish-yellow fat at temperatures of 18° to 20°C (65° to 68°F).

The flesh of the coconut, ground or grated, is widely used in confectionery and as a sweetening ingredient in a number of oriental dishes. Under-ripe coconuts provide a delicious milk. Another drink is obtained from the fermented sap (or *teddy*) and is known as palm wine. It is distilled to form an alcoholic drink called *arrack;* the thickened sap is called palm sugar (or jaggery).

Chicken Malái

1 × 15ml spoon (1 tablespoon) olive or vegetable oil
1 large onion, finely chopped
1 garlic clove, crushed
1 × 5ml spoon (1 teaspoon) ground turmeric
5cm (2in) root ginger, peeled and sliced, or pinch ground ginger
4 fresh or dried chilli peppers, de-seeded and chopped

6 cardamom seeds
6 cloves
1.25cm (1in) piece of cinnamon bark
500ml (18fl oz) thick coconut milk
salt
1.75kg (4lb) boiled chicken, skinned, boned and cut in slices

Heat the oil in a pan and gently fry the onion, garlic and spices until onion is soft, about 10 minutes. Add the hot coconut milk, salt and chicken pieces and simmer very gently for about 5 minutes. Remove cloves and cinnamon before serving.

Serves 6

Coriander

Coriandrum sativum L.

Coriander is an annual to biennial plant of the family Umbelliferae with erect stems branched in the upper part. It grows to about 20 to 70cm (8 to 28in) high. The bottom leaves are single-pinnate and the upper leaves are finely divided. Flowers are pinkish-mauve and the fruit is a pale brown, spherical indehisce-achene with a calyx at the top.

Coriander is probably indigenous to western Asia or the eastern Mediterranean. It is cultivated mainly in southern Europe, India, and South America. It has a long history and was mentioned in the Old Testament; it was used in ancient Rome both as a condiment and a medicament.

The ripe dry achenes are used for seasoning. They have a pleasant scent and a spicy, sweetish taste. Coriander should be kept in a tightly closed jar away from light, as the oil evaporates. Fresh young leaves can also be used as a seasoning. Coriander is used in making curries, and in seasoning stews and game. It also can be used to aromatize beer and vinegar. It goes well with smoked meat and pickled vegetables and is widely used in Indian, Latin American and Russian cooking.

The main component of the essential oils (up to 1 per cent) is linalool. It has phytoncidic effects, preventing bacteria from multiplying. Coriander stimulates the appetite, relieves flatulence and promotes gastric and intestinal function. It strengthens the nervous system. The fruits can be candied and chewed to freshen the breath.

Cornelian Cherry

Cornus mas L.

Cornelian Cherry is a branched-out shrub with erect twigs and ovate leaves in opposite arrangement. It grows up to 5m (15ft) high. The yellow flowers open in March and the fruits grow separately or in twos to fives on the twigs. They are oblong, barrel-shaped drupes, 1.5 to 2cm (1/2 to 3/4in) long, and carmine red in colour. Each fruit has one stone, and ripens in September. The Cornelian Cherry is native to southern Europe and the Black Sea region but is also found in central Europe on dry stony slopes.

Fresh or dried fruits are used as a seasoning, or stewed and preserved with cranberries, rowanberries and wild Maraschino cherries. In Trans-Caucasia they are dried and ground into a bitter-sour powder for seasoning barbecued meat. They are also made into brandy or, when dried, added to sauce served with game.

The drupes contain vitamins C and A, and many organic acids, tannins and pectins.

European Barberry

Berberis vulgaris L.

The European Barberry is a thorny shrub which grows up to 3m (9ft) high with serrate, longish ovate leaves arranged in clusters. The flowers are small and yellow, hanging in clusters. The fruits are egg-shaped bright red berries with a sour taste. They ripen in September and contain several drop-shaped seeds.

The Barberry is widespread in central and southern Europe and it can also be found in dry stony sites in eastern Europe. However, it is prone to disease and acts as a host to 'wheat rust' and therefore has to be cleared in some places.

Both the fresh and the dried fruit are used as seasoning. They contain vitamin C, carotene, organic acids and the alkaloid berberin. They act as a diuretic and mild laxative and stimulate the bile. Small amounts of Barberry are healthy; large doses irritate the kidneys.

The fruits are processed into juice, preserves and liqueurs, and may also be dried and ground into a powder used for seasoning barbecued meat and fish.

Cranberry

Vaccinium vitis-idaea L.

The Cranberry is a very low semi-shrub with evergreen, small ovate leaves. It has white or pale-pink, bell-shaped flowers in clusters. The fruit is a berry which is white at first and then turns red.

The Cranberry is found in Europe, America and Asia and grows in dry forests in sandy soil. The fruits are used as a seasoning and a medicament.

The berries can be stewed or preserved or dried and added as a flavouring to sauces which are usually served with game or poultry.

The berries contain a large quantity of vitamin C, arbutin, benzoic acid (which prevents decomposition), citric acid, pectins, sugars, the glycoside vacciniine, tannins and pigments. The berries help prevent diarrhoea and stimulate the bile, as well as acting as a disinfectant.

Left: *Cornus mas*
Centre: *Berberis vulgaris*
Right: *Vaccinium vitis-idaea*

Horn of Plenty

Craterellus cornucopioides Persoon

This mushroom forms funnel-shaped fruit-bodies up to 10cm (4in) high with wavy, convoluted margins, either lacerated or entire. It is either smooth or wrinkled, and blue-black on the surface and brown-black and hoary on the inside.

It grows in late summer and in autumn in deciduous and mixed forests, but mostly under beeches or oak trees. It is to be found all over central Europe, and grows in big clusters.

An ugly-looking mushroom, it nonetheless has a pleasant spicy smell and its fruit-bodies, dried and powdered, are used as a seasoning.

This mushroom can be used to flavour soups, sauces and stuffings. It can be eaten stewed with a mixture of other mushrooms. Fresh, it can be eaten in quite large quantities as it is quite mild, but is much stronger when dried and should be used only sparingly.

Stewed Mushrooms on Toast

50g (2oz) butter or olive oil
1 small onion, sliced
200g (8oz) mushrooms *(Craterellus cornucopioides)*, sliced

salt and pepper
1 teaspoon caraway seeds
1 × 15ml spoon (1 tablespoon) chopped parsley

Melt the butter in a pan, add the onion and fry gently until golden. Add the mushrooms, salt, caraway seed and pepper, and stew until the mushrooms are tender, about 8 minutes.
Serve on hot buttered toast or fried bread, and sprinkle with chopped parsley.

Serves 4

Saffron

Crocus sativus L.

Saffron is a plant of the family Iridaceae. It has a scaly underground corm about the size of a walnut, from which linear leaves with white central nerves sprout in the spring. Saffron flowers from September to November (unlike decorative crocuses which flower in early spring). The flower is violet in colour, with six petals. The typical pistil has an inferior ovary and style branched out into three tubular, orange-coloured stigmas, enlarged at the end. The dried stigmas provide the seasoning.

Saffron has been famous for centuries, not only as a seasoning but also as a medicament, a perfume and a dye. Its cultivation spread many centuries ago from western Asia to India, China and then westwards to the Mediterranean. The oldest tradition of cultivation in Europe is in southern France and in Spain. The ancient Egyptians, Romans and Greeks used Saffron a great deal.

Saffron is used as a culinary herb in soups, sauces and cheeses. It adds colour as well as taste and is also used in rice dishes.

The flowers are collected in autumn, in the early morning. The stigmas with a part of the style are plucked out and dried in the sun or by artificial heat. Saffron is very costly to grow as, in the first year of cultivation, one hectare (2.471 acres) only yields about 6 kg (13lb) of dried saffron. It also requires a large amount of manpower to collect it and it is beginning to be replaced by cheaper substitutes, for example the flowers of the Safflower *(Carthamus tintorius)*.

Tchikhirtma (Lamb Soup)
(Caucasia)

500g (1lb) boned lamb	1 × 2.5ml spoon (1/2 teaspoon) saffron
1 × 15ml spoon (1 tablespoon) butter	2 × 5ml spoons (2 teaspoons) lemon juice
2 onions, chopped	3 egg yolks
1 × 15ml spoon (1 tablespoon) flour	1 × 15ml spoon (1 tablespoon)
salt	chopped fresh coriander or parsley
pepper	

Put the lamb in a pan, cover with cold water and bring to the boil. Cover and simmer until tender. Remove the meat from the stock and cut it into 2.5cm (1in) pieces.

Melt the butter in a pan, add the onion and fry until tender. Stir in the flour and cook slowly for 2 minutes, stirring all the time. Add the meat, stock, salt, pepper, saffron and lemon juice. Bring to the boil and simmer for 10 minutes. Just before serving, blend together the egg yolks and a little of the hot stock. Return the egg mixture to the pan and reheat but do not boil. Sprinkle the soup with coriander or parsley.

Serves 4

Cumin

Cuminum cyminum L.

Cumin is an annual plant belonging to the carrot family, Umbelliferae, and resembling Caraway. The flowers, which are arranged in umbels, are off-white or reddish, and the fruits are grey-green achenes, larger than Caraway seeds, and marked by volatile oil channels.

Cumin was well known in ancient Egypt: it has been found in the Pyramids. In those days it was more widely used as a medicinal plant. It is indigenous to Ethiopia and at present is cultivated in India, eastern and southern Europe, and North Africa.

Only the dry achenes, whole or ground, are used as a seasoning. Ground cumin is a greenish-brown colour, with a pungent aroma and sharp taste.

Cumin is a regular component of curry powder and is widely used in Indian and Eastern cooking. It is included in mixed spices and added to stews and grilled meats. In the Netherlands and North America it is used in cheeses, smoked products and canned food.

Cumin contains approximately 3 per cent of essential oil (different in composition to that of Caraway) and bitter principles along with other substances with an astringent taste. It stimulates the appetite and the digestive juices and acts as a carminative. It is used in the production of digestion liqueurs.

122

Turmeric (also known as Curcuma)

Curcuma longa L., syn. *Curcuma domestica* L.

This tropical herbaceous plant belongs to the family Zingiberaceae. It reaches a height of 60 to 100cm (24 to 40in). The leaves are elliptical and elongate, and the flowers are yellow. It is grown for its rhizomes and thickened roots which are sometimes known as 'yellow ginger'.

Turmeric is native to south-eastern Asia and is cultivated today in China, India, Java, Haiti and the Malagasy Republic and in the Phillippines and Japan. The harvested rootstalks are cleaned, scalded with hot water and dried in the sun.

The dried rootstalks, or the powdered form, were known in Europe centuries ago – Turmeric was described by Dioscorides. Presumably it was first brought to Europe by Arab merchants and, in the Middle Ages, the Europeans knew it under the name of 'Indian Saffron'. In those days, its use was more specifically as a medicine and a cloth dye than as a seasoning.

The distinct, spicy taste and aroma of Turmeric make it an ideal condiment for hot sauces, mustard and curry powders.

Turmeric contains a volatile oil with a characteristic sharp smell and a bright yellow pigment, curcumin. This pigment is the basic component of the rootstalks and is used to colour food and for dying fabrics and wood. Turmeric is insoluble in water but dissolves in fat and alcohol. A Turmeric infusion is supposed to be good for the stomach and is helpful as a treatment for kidney and bile disorders. It can also be applied externally as a disinfectant. The oil is used in perfumery.

Lemon Grass (also known as **Citronella**)

Cymbopogon flexuosus (Steudel) Watson

There are some 30 species of perennial grasses which are classified in the genus *Cymbopogon (Andropogon)*. They are members of the family Graminae (grasses). Several of these grasses are known as Lemon Grass. In fact, all the grasses in this group are very similar to each other, although they yield different essential oils; the blades, sheaths, leaves, husks and rhizomes of all these species have cells which exude an aromatic oil.

Lemon Grass contains essential oils reminiscent in both taste and smell of Lemon and Lemon Balm. It can either be used as a seasoning or for the manufacture of oil in pharmaceutical and perfume industry.

Lemon Grass grows in tropical and sub-tropical regions and was used centuries ago by the Egyptians, Romans and Greeks, mainly for cosmetic and medicinal purposes.

As a seasoning, it is used mainly in Indonesian and Indian cuisine. It is added, with other ingredients, to marinades for grilled meat and is one of the ingredients in a special paste used in Indonesian cooking. The fresh or dried greenery can be used in any dish where a lemony scent is required, but a large pinch is probably enough to flavour a dish for four people.

Lemon Grass contains the essential oils citral and geraniol, in differing quantities; they are yellowish to brownish and have a lemon-like scent. In small quantities, the oil aids digestion, increases the secretion of bile, prevents flatulence and helps reduce blood pressure, as well as acting as a sedative.

In cool climates, Lemon Grass (or Citronella, as it is sometimes known) can be grown in pots in warm greenhouses or indoors. Since it does not flower or bear fruit in such conditions, it must be propagated vegetatively.

Cardamom

Elettaria cardamomum (L.) Maton,
syn. *Amomum cardamomum* L.

Cardamom is native to the rain forests of India, Ceylon, Sumatra and China. The thick underground rhizome sends out tall stems with oblong, lanceolate foliage. Later on, out of the same rootstalk, grow the flower-bearing stalks. These bear short clusters of flowers. The fruits are ovate or oblong capsules about 1 to 2cm (1/2 to 3/4in) long, containing a large number of crosswise grooved seeds.

The seeds of Cardamom were used as a seasoning and medicament by the Greeks and Romans. In western Europe, Cardamom is not common as a seasoning but it has always been popular in the Far East, where it is also added to tea and coffee.

The ripe fruit capsules are dried either in the sun or artificially. They are cleaned and graded and sometimes sulphurized to bleach them. The seeds have a strong, camphor-like smell and pungent taste. They contain 4 to 8 per cent of cardamom essential oil and 10 per cent of oil, resin and starch. They are used in medicines or as a seasoning.

As a seasoning, they are added to pastry and sweets, and to smoked products and various spice mixtures. They are also used in the manufacture of liqueurs.

Apart from the true Cardamom, seeds of many related species are used in the same way.

Black Coffee Spiced with Cardamom

1 cup strong black coffee   sugar, if required
3 to 4 Cardamom seeds, whole or
ground

You can either add ground Cardamom to ready-made coffee or you can add the Cardamom grains when you are making the coffee. Add sugar to taste.

Garden Rocket

Eruca sativa Miller

The Garden Rocket belongs to the family Cruciferae. Its average height is about 80cm (32in). The stem is either glabrous or sparsely pubescent and the leaves are lyre-shaped, digitate-pinnate with dentate margins — the upper leaves are usually sessile and undivided. Garden Rocket flowers from June to July and the flowers are pale yellow with purple venation. The fruits are siliquas which adhere to the axis of the raceme. They are erect and small with a short, sword-shaped tip. The seeds are small, brown and smooth.

Garden Rocket grows in the wild around the Mediterranean and in Afghanistan. It is cultivated both in Asia and Europe, and is used in French cuisine.

The seeds contain about 30 per cent of a pungent oil which is pressed and used in industry as well as in cooking.

In India, the oil, which is golden yellow to golden brown in colour, is used to make a solution for pickling vegetables, but it loses its pungency after six months. The young shoots can be used fresh as a flavouring for salads. They can also be used to garnish canapés and cold meat, and for flavouring spreads. They can be made into a piquant salad or used with other vegetables in mixed salads.

Like a number of other similar herbs, Garden Rocket contains a high proportion of vitamin C and mineral salt, organic acids and medicinal substances. It is reputed to be good for curing vitamin C deficiency at the end of winter.

Giant Fennel

Ferula assa-foetida L.

This is a stout, perennial herb of the carrot family, Umbelliferae, with a thickened, beet-like root. It does not flower for several years, and forms a huge rosette of leaves up to 1m (3ft) long. The leaves are multiple-pinnate with narrow segments. After several years, the plant produces a strong, very tall stem, branched into whorls, with a large number of umbels composed of yellow-green flowers. After the flowering period, which lasts for six weeks, the fruits — brown achenes — are formed. A milky juice with a distinctive sharp smell is produced in the root; this juice is known as asafoetida.

Giant Fennel is indigenous to the sandy, arid plains of Iran, Afghanistan and India. A resinous juice is obtained by making incisions on the upper part of the root, and the juice solidifies on contact with the air. The grains or lumps of resin are grey-yellow at first and then turn red-brown. They have a sharp bitter taste and smell of garlic.

Giant Fennel contains essential oils, resins, gummy substances and other constituents. It is used as a medicine in the Far East. It acts as an anti-spasmodic and stimulates the alimentary tract, improving digestion. It also acts as a sedative. It must be administered in small doses.

Ragout of Beef with Vegetables

3 × 15ml spoons (3 tablespoons) olive oil
2 onions, chopped
2 green peppers, de-seeded and chopped
500g (1lb) stewing beef, cut into 2.5cm (1in) cubes
100g (4oz) tomato purée
2 × 15ml spoons (2 tablespoons) Worcester sauce
2 bay leaves
1 × 5ml spoon (1 teaspoon) cayenne pepper
2 cloves garlic, crushed
salt
black pepper
200g (7oz) mushrooms, sliced
100g (4oz) almonds, chopped
3 × 15ml spoons (3 tablespoons) olive oil

Heat the oil in a pan, add the onions, peppers and meat, and fry quickly until the meat is browned, turning once. Add the tomato purée, Worcester sauce, bay leaves, garlic, salt, pepper and mushrooms. Cover and simmer gently until meat is tender. Add a little stock or water from time to time if the mixture becomes too dry.
In a small pan, toss the almonds in oil until lightly coloured. Sprinkle the ragout with browned almonds and serve with saffron rice.

Serves 4

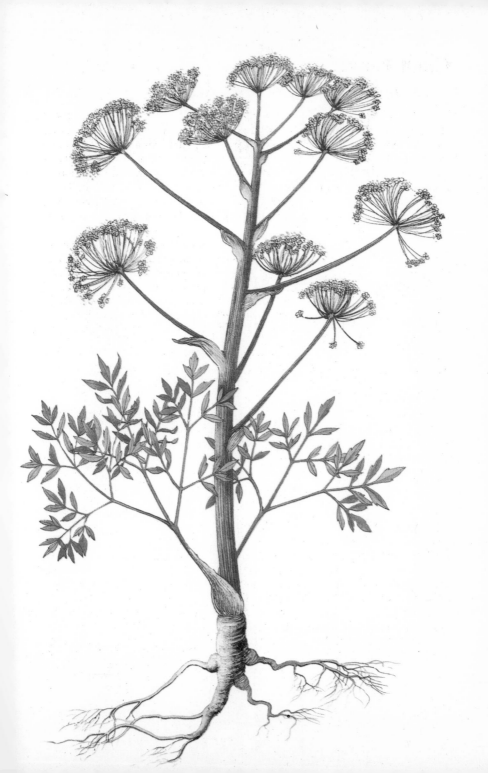

Fennel

Foeniculum vulgare Miller

True Fennel is a biennial plant which, in the right conditions, will grow for 3 to 4 years. It belongs to the family Umbelliferae. The stem reaches a height of about 1.5 to 2m (4 to 6ft). The leaves are four-merous with filiform segments and long, membraneous sheaths. The inflorescence is large and rich and the yellow flowers are arranged in flat umbels. It flowers in July and August, the whole plant resembling Dill, with a strong, sweet smell. The fruits are green or greenish-yellow to brownish achenes with a strong scent and a pleasant, slightly sweet taste.

The plant is found wild in southern Europe and is commonly cultivated in warm regions, in Europe, India, Japan and elsewhere. There are several varieties and the one most commonly grown in France, Sweet Fennel, is often used as a vegetable. The parts used for seasoning are the achenes and the young leaves; in Sweet Fennel, the petioles are also used. Good quality Fennel should be pale in colour with a strong scent.

Fennel seeds, ground or whole, are used for fresh or preserved vegetables, and, in spice mixtures, to flavour soups, sauces and pastries. In Italy, Fennel seeds are used to spice game. The fresh tops can be used in fish soups (as in France) and to add flavour to butter, cheeses and cheese spreads. The fruits are also used in the manufacture of liqueurs.

The fruits contain an essential oil with carminative properties and stimulate the appetite and intestinal activity.

Fennel can be grown wherever the summer is long, dry and warm. It needs lime-rich humid soil and plenty of light. It can be sown in a garden or in pots.

Woodruff

Galium odoratum (L.) Scopoli, syn. *Asperula odorata* L.

This perennial herbaceous plant of the family Rubiaceae has thin, creeping rhizomes sending out square, hairless stems with whorls of lanceolate leaves and corresponding stipules. The stems are topped by panicles of white, fragrant flowers with four-lobed corollas. The fruit is an achene covered with tiny, hook-like thorns. Woodruff, which flowers from April to May, is a melliferous plant and, when withering, has a smell rather like new-mown hay.

Woodruff grows in Europe and North America. It is found in central Europe in deciduous woods, usually of beech. Woodruff has been used since the 9th century by Benedictine monks as a seasoning and medicinal drug.

The young shoots are used as a seasoning; the fresh stems are usually picked in the flowering stage or just before full bloom in May. Woodruff is used when slightly faded, when it is at its most fragrant. Dried Woodruff should be pale green with a spicy, somewhat tart flavour.

Woodruff is used as an aromatizing agent in drinks, jellies, custards, teas and herbal liqueurs. It is also used to make a special punch known as May bowl, in which 2 or 3 fresh stems of Woodruff are marinated in a litre ($1^{1}/_{2}$ pints) of white wine for about 3 hours, and then removed just before serving. It is also good as a flavouring for cold milk with honey or for cider. Woodruff should not be chopped or cut before being added to drinks or food, but marinated whole.

It contains coumarin, glycosides, asperulosid, bitter principles, tannins, fats, sugars and fenolic substances. It stimulates the digestion and metabolism, and strengthens and calms the body. However, in large doses, it can cause dizziness and headaches.

It can be gathered in the wild or cultivated by planting seedlings or setting out offshoots. It should be grown in semi-shaded soil, which is light, loose and humus-rich.

Ground Ivy

Glechoma hederacea L.

A perennial plant of the family Labiatae, Ground Ivy grows to about 10 to 30cm (4 to 12in) high with a creeping rootstalk. The stems are climbing, and the hairless leaves are small, reniform to cordiform, resembling those of ivy. Flowers grow in leaf axils and are bluish, purplish or pink-tinted, occasionally white. Ground Ivy flowers from April to September.

Ground Ivy has been used in cooking since the Middle Ages. It was supposed to ward off the plague and bewitchment. It grows wild in Europe and Asia.

Since Ground Ivy can be found almost anywhere in the wild, it is not usually cultivated. The young stems, with the leaves and flowers, are cut off near the ground, preferably in April, May or July. The scent is aromatic and the taste bitter and spicy. Both fresh and dried leaves and stalks, together with the flowers, are used for seasoning. Good quality seasoning should be grey-green coloured, never brownish. Ground Ivy should be dried carefully, and stored in closed jars, away from light.

Ground Ivy is used mainly fresh in soups (particularly potato and vegetable), egg dishes, stuffings and herbal butters and cheeses. Dried Ground Ivy is added to dried herbal mixtures and to soups, casseroles, hamburgers and sauces.

The stalks and leaves of the plant contain the bitter principle glechomin, essential oils, tannins, resins, cholin and vitamins. It improves the metabolism and affects the urinary passages. It is a healing agent in diseases of the respiratory tract.

Easter Meat Loaf
(Czechoslovakia)

250g (9oz) boiled smoked meat
400g (14oz) mixed cooked white meat
   (pork or veal)
6 eggs, lightly beaten
salt
pepper
6 slices white bread
2 × 15ml spoons (2 tablespoons) butter

2 × 15ml spoons (2 tablespoons)
   Ground Ivy
2 × 15ml spoons (2 tablespoons) young
   nettles
1 × 15ml spoon (1 tablespoon) chives
2 × 15ml spoons (2 tablespoons) parsley
2 × 15ml spoons (2 tablespoons) milk

Dice the meat into small cubes and make the bread into breadcrumbs. Mix together in a bowl. Mix the milk with the melted butter, the salt, the eggs and the finely chopped herbs. Then add to the meat and breadcrumbs and mix in well. Grease a baking tin (a loaf tin, for example), add the mixture and cover with foil. Cook in a moderate oven for approximately 1 hour. Serve hot or cold.

Serves 4 to 6

Soya Bean
Glycine max (L.) Merrill

The Soya Bean is an annual plant of the genus *Glycine* of the family Papilionaceae. Most species of this genus grow in the wild in the tropics, but the cultivated Soya Bean is a hybrid formed many centuries ago.

The Soya Bean is cultivated in China and Japan in particular. It is an extremely useful source of proteins and oil and has been used widely in the food and chemical industries. It is processed into a number of different products — flour, oil, lecithin, milk, cheese, spicy sauce and paste and cattle fodder, for example. The young pods can be eaten as a vegetable.

The ripe seeds contain up to 60 per cent proteins and 20 per cent oil. Indeed, its protein and fat content is so high that 300g (11oz) of soya flour are equivalent to the calorific value of 27 eggs. Recently a new constituent, known as cytelin, has been found in Soya Beans; this is supposed to have a healing effect on arteriosclerosis.

The oil from Soya Beans forms the basic cooking oil used in Asia. Soya sauce is used widely in Asian and Chinese cooking. It is made by a fermentation process from Soya Beans and cornflour. It is a dark brown, thick liquid and improves with keeping — like wine, the older the vintage the better.

Oriental Fried Meat

500g (1lb) of pork, beef, lamb or
  chicken
4 × 15ml spoons (4 tablespoons) oil
2 × 15ml spoons (2 tablespoons) wine
2 × 14ml spoons (2 tablespoons)
  soya sauce

sugar
1 star anise
black pepper
pinch monosodium glutamate (optional)
salt

Cut meat into bite-sized pieces. Fry in the oil until browned on all sides. Add wine, soya sauce, the star anise and a pinch of sugar, black pepper and monosodium glutamate, if desired. Simmer gently, uncovered, until the meat is tender.

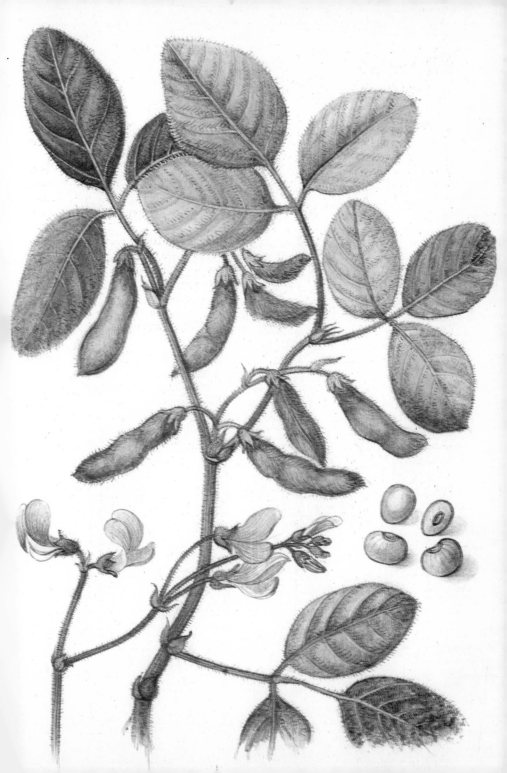

Liquorice

Glycyrrhiza glabra L.

This is a perennial plant of the family Papilionaceae. It grows up to 180cm (52in) high, with a woody rhizome reaching 1 to 2m (3 to 6ft) in length. It sends out erect stems with odd-pinnate leaves and blue-purple flowers collected into clusters. It flowers in June and July. The fruits are hairless legumes with 3 to 5 seeds.

Liquorice originates from the eastern Mediterranean and the Near East. It has become established in southern Europe and in southern parts of eastern Europe. It is also found in western and south-western Asia. In the warmer regions of central Europe, its cultivation is being extended, mainly for pharmaceutical purposes.

The rootstalks (known as 'sweetroot') are used for seasoning and medicinal purposes. They have a faint smell and a sweetish taste. They are covered by a brownish bark, and the peeled rhizomes are sulphur yellow. Liquorice is used pulverized. The rhizomes and roots are harvested in the third or fourth year after planting, either in the autumn or early spring. The cleaned and washed roots are dried at temperatures of 35°C (95°F) and then peeled to remove the resinous substances.

The thickened and processed extract of liquorice is used in confectionery, usually sold as liquorice sticks – a rubber-like substance, dark greyish-brown in colour.

Liquorice contains up to 15 per cent of glycyrrhizine, glycosides, essential oil, tannins, potassium, calcium, flavone substances and phytoncides. It has an antispasmodic effect and reduces irritability of the stomach. Applied externally, the extract has special anti-inflammatory properties. Liquorice affects the secretion of the gastric juices and has a diuretic effect. It is also a carminative and eliminates spasms of the intestinal tract. It has hormonal effects, and is used in the treatment of duodenal ulcers. It helps improve the metabolism but if taken for too long can lead to the retention of water in the body.

Four varieties are cultivated: *typica, violacea, glandulifera* and *pallida*. Liquorice must be grown in a sunny, dry place in a medium to light clay soil, rich in nutrients. It is propagated by cuttings taken from the base of the plant. They should have several buds and be about 20cm (8in) long.

Hibiscus
(also known as **Indian Sorrel** or **Red Sorrel**)
Hibiscus sabdariffa L.

Hibiscus is probably native to India and is grown in many tropical regions for different purposes. It exists in many varieties, some of them cultivated for their pink or red calyxes which have a sourish taste, and others for their leaves and seeds. It belongs to the family Malvaceae and has yellow flowers and a long, lobed stem with the leaves on the lowest part. It needs high temperatures and constant humidity to grow well.

The calyxes are dried in the sun and used for making a sourish, red-tinted drink, served either hot like tea or chilled like lemonade. It is also used as an ingredient in various dishes and syrups. It is popular in Indian and Arab countries.

Okra
Hibiscus esculentus L.

This plant, which is closely related to *H. sabdariffa,* reaches a height of 1 to 3m (3 to 9ft) and has large five-lobed leaves with venation on the underside. The fruits are capsules, 6 to 20cm ($2^{1}/_{2}$ to 8in) long, pointed and furrowed at the sides.

In this species, which is probably native to India, the fruits are collected unripe just as the seeds begin to develop. They are used in various dishes, aromatic soups and sauces and in some areas the dried and roasted seeds are used as a substitute for coffee. Okra is very popular in Arab cooking.

Sea Buckthorn

Hippophae rhamnoides L.

This is a thorny dioecious shrub about 2m (6ft) high. The young branches have silvery scales and the leaves are narrow, and silver-grey on the underside. The small male flowers form short catkins while the female flowers, which are equally small, are arranged in clusters. The fruits are small oval drupes, yellow to dark orange in colour. Sea Buckthorn is often cultivated on poor, dry soil as an ornamental shrub.

It is found in southern Europe and the southern slopes of the Caucasus and Trans-Caucasia. It is planted as an ornamental shrub in central Europe. The ripe fruits are processed for seasoning purposes and sold either dried or made into pastes, syrups, juices or jams.

Dried or ground fruits can be sprinkled over barbecued meat. Fresh fruits are added to sauces accompanying game. The fruit can be added to all dishes in which lemon is used, but only at the end of cooking time. The fresh fruit should not come into contact with metal.

The vitamin content of Sea Buckthorn is very high, particularly vitamin C and A. Organic acids and the glycoside quercetin are also present and vitamin C is also contained in the leaves. Sea Buckthorn improves the appetite, acts as a tonic and helps prevent infection.

To make sure the plant fruits, a male plant must be grown near female ones. It is not particularly difficult to grow and will do well on dry, sunny, sandy soil. The fruits mature and are harvested from August to October.

Jew's Ear

Hirneola auricula-judae (St. Amans) Berkeley

Jew's Ear is a fungus found on trunks of the Black Elder *(Sambucus nigra)* as a saprophyte of dead wood and bark. In damp weather it forms aggregate fruit-bodies which are cup- or shell-shaped, irregularly curved and lobed, often in the shape of ear lobes. They are found in clusters, and are thin, leathery and resilient. Normally chestnut-brown in colour and slightly transparent, they turn black-brown and hard in dry weather, returning to their former shape when wet.

It grows throughout the year, but mainly from August to March. It is not much used in Europe but a popular edible mushroom in China, Japan and New Zealand.

Shii-take

Lentinus edodes (Berkeley) Singer

This is a delicious edible fungus, found growing in the wild in the sub-tropical regions and temperate zones of eastern Asia. It is now artificially cultivated, mainly in Japan. It grows on the wood of various deciduous trees and the caps reach 5 to 10cm (2 to 4in) in diameter. They are usually left to dry for about 24 hours after picking.

They can be used fresh and dried, and are also preserved in cans and pastes. They have a beneficial effect on the human body, reducing cholesterol levels and slowing down the process of arteriosclerosis.

Mu-sü-jou
(China)

250g (9oz) pork fillet
1 × 15ml spoon (1 tablespoon) soy sauce
1 × 5ml spoon (1 teaspoon) cornflour
2 × 15ml spoons (2 tablespoons) vegetable oil
1 onion, chopped
1 × 5ml spoon (1 teaspoon) sugar

1 × 15ml spoon (1 tablespoon) brandy
50ml (2oz) water
30g (1oz) dried Jew's Ear mushrooms, chopped and soaked
2 eggs, scrambled
salt
pepper

Cut the pork into thin strips. Add soy sauce and cornflour, mix well and leave to stand for an hour. Heat the oil in a pan, add the pork mixture, onion, sugar and brandy. Once the pork has browned, add the mushrooms and water and stir-fry quickly until tender. Add the scrambled eggs and season with salt and pepper. Serve with rice.

Serves 2

Top: *Hirneola auricula-judae*
Bottom: *Lentinus edodes*

Hop

Humulus lupulus L.

This twining, dioecious plant of the family Cannabaceae has stems reaching a length of up to 6m (18ft). The leaves are palmate. Only the female plants, which form cone-like flowers covered by golden lupulin glands, are cultivated.

The Wild Hop grows in thickets along brooks, in lowland woods and ditches, in most parts of Europe. The plant is cultivated principally for the production of beer but it has been used as a medicinal herb and seasoning for centuries.

The Romans used Hop shoots as a vegetable — they were eaten in salad with a vinaigrette dressing. The young shoots can also be cooked like asparagus. The flowers or cones (the hops) used to be added to soups.

Hyssop

Hyssopus officinalis L.

Hyssop is a perennial, branched shrub of the family Labiatae, usually about 60cm (24in) high. The square stems are covered by linear, dark green leaves. The flowers are usually bluish-purple, but may also be pink and white, and are clustered in leaf axils. It is a decorative plant, flowering from July to September. It is aromatic and melliferous.

Hyssop is native to the Mediterranean coast and to central Asia. It has now become widely established in western Asia as well. It is widely cultivated in most Arab countries. Hyssop was first introduced into central Europe in the 10th century by Benedictine monks, and was grown in monastery gardens.

The young leaves, either fresh or dried, are used as a seasoning and the fleshy parts of the stems can be picked in the early flowering stage and dried. Dry Hyssop is a grey-green colour. Make sure that any leaves used are not damaged by rust. Hyssop has a spicy and camphor-like scent and a slightly bitter, but quite pleasant taste.

Hyssop has a wide range of culinary uses and can be added to most dishes. It goes particularly well with all types of vegetables and pulses, cheese spreads and dips, mayonnaise, herbal butter and salads, but can be used equally well to flavour game and beef, stuffings and meat balls. In the East, fermented Hyssop leaves are used to make a mildly alcoholic drink called 'sherbet'. Dried Hyssop can be used in the same way as fresh Hyssop for cooking.

The stems and leaves of the plant contain essential oils (pinocamphen, pinen), the flavonoid glycoside hesperidin, approximately 8 per cent tannins, the pigment hysopin, and other principles. Hyssop has germicidal properties. The fresh leaves have a high percentage of vitamin C. Hyssop is supposed to improve digestion, stimulate the appetite and reduce sweating. It is also used to ease coughs, by acting as an expectorant.

Hyssop is easy to cultivate, either in the garden or in boxes. It makes a good ornamental perennial as well as a useful herb. It needs light, lime-rich soil and can be sown directly into the bed or grown from pre-cultivated seedlings. It can be prepared by dividing clumps of the plant. If the plant is to be used fresh, both the stalks and leaves can be cut just before flowering, but if it is to be dried, only the stripped leaves should be used.

Star Anise (also known as Chinese Anise)

Illicium verum Hooker

The Star Anise is a small evergreen tree of the family Magnoliaceae. It reaches an average height of 8m (24ft) and has smooth, dense branches covered by grey bark. The flowers are pale yellow-green and have a distinct fragrance. The spice called Star or Chinese Anise is the dried aggregate fruit, consisting of one-seeded follicles with glossy, smooth seeds. When ripe, the follicles turn brown and woody. They grow in formations of 6 to 10, creating symmetrical, star-like shapes. The stars are usually eight-lobed and split on the upper side.

Star Anise is native to southern China, where it is still cultivated today. Its range extends to Japan and the Phillippines and it is also found elsewhere in the tropics. Star Anise tastes very similar to aniseed, and is pleasantly spicy and sweetish, but has a rather more delicate flavour.

In cooking, the fruits are used as a condiment, particularly in Asiatic cuisine. In Europe, Star Anise is added to pastry, stewed fruit and plum jam.

Star Anise contains 4 to 5 per cent fine and fragrant essential oil with the substance anethol. The oil from Star Anise is processed industrially to make liqueurs and perfumery. It was also used as a sedative and tonic in the past, while today it is used as a flavouring in medicinal teas and syrups.

Illicium religiosum

A related species, the fruits of which closely resemble Star Anise but which are poisonous, is cultivated in Japan. It is grown for decoration and planted around temples.

Chinese Pork

500g (1lb) pork fillet	pinch each of hot pepper, ground ginger, curry powder
1 onion	
2 cloves garlic	1 star anise, ground
2 × 15ml spoons (2 tablespoons) oil	2 peppers (or 1 leek)
2 × 15ml spoons (2 tablespoons) dried, macerated mushrooms	1 tomato
	pinch salt
2 × 15ml spoon (2 tablespoons) soya sauce	

Cut the meat into thin strips, fry in the oil to brown and add the garlic and onion. Cook until the onion is soft. Add the remaining ingredients and stir-fry until all the ingredients are tender. Serve with rice.

Serves 4

Common Juniper

Juniperus communis L.

This is a coniferous shrub or a branched small tree of the Cupressaceae family, reaching a height of 3m (9ft). The grey-green needles, which are short and tough, are arranged, whorl-like, in threes. The Juniper is an evergreen dioecious plant. The bark is smooth to begin with, and then peels. The male flowers are yellow and resemble cones, while the female flowers are greenish and bud-like. Juniper flowers from April to May. The spherical fruits are green in the first year and dark russet to purple-blue in the second. The plant has a pleasant, resinous smell.

Common Juniper grows on dry hillsides, in pine forests on sandy soil, and even on poor rocky soil, in mountainous regions throughout the northern hemisphere.

The ripe, dried fruits, or berries, are used as a seasoning, mainly in Europe. They should be red-brown to blue-black in colour, with a spicy aroma. Both the berries and the wood provide a medicinal drug.

The berries are used as a condiment in cooking and in marinating game, in sauces, and in sauerkraut. They are also used in goulash and when roasting fat poultry. Juniper berries can be used to make up mixed spices: together with coriander, they are used in curing smoked meat, for example. The berries are also widely used for flavouring alcoholic drinks, such as gin and juniper brandy.

The fruits contain inosit, flavonoid, glycosides, the bitter juniperin, and are 30 per cent inert sugar and 9 per cent resin. The essential oil containing terpenes, which stimulates the activity of the kidneys, is the most important medicinal ingredient. The disinfectant phytoncides are also present. The berries have a diuretic effect, and affect the blood flow in the mucous membrane of the digestive tract. They also have carminative and anti-rheumatic properties and improve blood circulation. Juniper berries should not be taken by people suffering from kidney inflammation, or by pregnant women.

Juniper can be grown easily from seed, or from young plants with developed roots. The male plants grow more upright than the female ones. The berries are collected in the wild from September to October. They are dried in a thin layer in a temperature which must not exceed 35°C (95°F), otherwise the essential oil evaporates.

Orange Agaric

Lactarius deliciosus L.

This best-known representative of the genus *Lactarius* has an orange-reddish fruit-body. The cap has an incurved edge, and in old age it is often funnel-shaped. The skin of the cap is smooth or even slimy, and its surface is striped with more or less conspicuous concentric rings which are coloured greenish. The stipe is cylindrical, hollow, the same colour as the cap. The flesh is white and brittle. When cut or bruised, the whole fruit-body produces carrot-orange milk which turns green when it dries. The gills also turn green when bruised.

Orange Agaric grows in grass and moss both in coniferous and broadleaved forests throughout Europe. Usually a larger number of fruit-bodies is found growing together.

It is a much sought-after, deliciously tasting mushroom of brittle consistence, with a characteristic spicy, pleasant flavour and smell.

In the kitchen, it can be used in many different ways and in any quantity. It is particularly good for sauces, with roast or stewed meat, in ragôuts, goulash or in mushroom soups. Its flavour is best when it is pickled in vinegar with onion.

Sauce from Orange Agarics

50 g (2oz) butter
1 onion
500 g (1lb) orange agarics
salt
1×5 ml spoon (1 teaspoon) curry
1×15 ml spoon (1 tablespoon) chopped parsley

pinch caraway seeds
1 clove garlic
200 g (8oz) cream
2 × 5 ml spoons (2 tablespoons) lemon juice
1×15 ml spoon (1 talbespoon) flour
water or stock

Chop the onion and fry quickly in butter. Add curry, caraway seeds and finely chopped orange agarics. Sprinkle with salt and cook until tender. Then add crushed garlic and let simmer for a short while. Add flour and a glass of water or stock. Stir in the cream, add parsley and lemon juice. The sauce should be quite thick. It is served, either warm or cold, with boiled meat (beef, fish or poultry), as well as with grilled and roast meat (pork cutlets, chicken, steak or fish). It is also good with game.

Pepper Mushroom
(also known as **Milk Mushroom**)
Lactarius piperatus (Swartz) Fries

This mushroom has a cap about 6 to 20cm ($2^{1}/_{2}$ to 8in) in diameter, white or yellowish in colour (but brownish if older or bruised). The cap is dry and smooth. In young mushrooms it is convex but in older mushrooms it turns into a concave funnel-shape with an incurved edge. The gills are white, very dense and short, with slightly yellowing edges. The stipe is cylindrical, relatively short and thick, white and smooth. The flesh is white, firm, hard and brittle and produces a large quantity of white milk when cut. The milk has an astringent taste.

The Pepper Mushroom grows abundantly in all types of forests and can be found even in dry weather when other mushrooms are scarce. It grows in the whole temperate zone of the northern hemisphere and also in Australia.

It has an unusual flavour which not everyone finds agreeable, but as a condiment, dried and crushed, it has a good flavour. The mushroom is popular in the eastern Carpathian region where the local inhabitants pick it in preference to other mushrooms and preserve it.

The related, bitter tasting Sharp Agaric *(L. terminosus)* can also be eaten, provided it is cooked first in salted water to remove some of its bitterness.

Chicken with Vegetables and Mushrooms

1 chicken breast
100g (4oz) mushrooms
2 to 3 red peppers
200g (7oz) leek
2 × 15ml spoons (2 tablespoons) dessert wine
1 × 5ml spoon (1 teaspoon) soya sauce

2 × 15ml spoons (2 tablespoons) oil
1 small onion
pinch cayenne pepper
pinch ginger
salt
1 × 5ml spoon (1 teaspoon) cornflour
50ml (2fl oz) stock

Cut the chicken and peppers into thin strips. Chop the vegetables and mushrooms. Fry the peppers and leeks in hot oil and remove them. Mix the chicken with the onion, fry it quickly and, stirring continuously, add the mushrooms, seasoning, soya sauce, wine, and the stock mixed with the cornflour. Stir and stew until the mixture is tender. Add the fried vegetables, stew for a few more minutes, salt according to taste. Serve with dry, unsalted rice.

Serves 4

Bay (also known as **Laurel Bay** or **Sweet Bay**)
Laurus nobilis L.

This member of the Lauraceae family is a shrub or small tree with evergreen, leathery leaves of an oblong, ovate to lanceolate shape. Some of them have a crinkly edge. They are glossy green above and paler below with a pronounced venation. They are usually 6 to 8cm (2½ to 3½in) long and about 2 to 4cm (1 to 1¾in) wide. The bay has whitish to yellowish flowers and the fruit is a red-blue berry with one seed.

Bay grows in the Mediterranean, in the Black Sea area, in the Trans-Caucasian region and in Iran, as well as in other sub-tropical zones. It is widely cultivated in Europe and was well known in ancient times when it was used in particular for making wreaths. It is still used for the same purpose today.

For culinary purposes only the leaves are used, usually dried. They have a strong scent and a slightly bitter taste. Good-quality dried leaves should be unbroken, supple and pale green. Brownish, brittle leaves are old and of poor quality. The leaves can be used whole or ground, but should never be kept for longer than two years because they lose their flavour after this time. They should be stored in a dry, tightly closed container and protected from light.

As a seasoning, Bay has been used for a long time in European, Arab, and South American cuisine. It is usually added to pickles of different types and, with other herbs and spices, to stews, ragouts and soups. It is also added to cream sauces.

The leaves contain essential oils, glycosides and bitter principles, which promote digestion and improve the appetite. The fruits are pressed to make laurel oil which is used in medicine.

Bay is generally cultivated as a shrub in warm areas near the sea. It can also be grown at home in pots and does not need particularly good soil. The leaves are picked in the autumn and dried in thin layers in the shade.

Lavender

Lavandula spica L., syn.*Lavandula angustifolia* Miller,
Lavandula officinalis Chaix

Lavender is a perennial branched semi-shrub of the Labiatae family which grows up to 80cm (32in) high, with linear sessile foliage. The leaves are felted at first and then turn green with glandular dots during their growth. The flowers are blue to purple-blue, arranged in spikes. The flowering time is from June to August and the fruits are mericarpia. All parts of the Lavender have a characteristic, pleasant strong scent.

Lavender is indigenous to the west coast of the Mediterranean. It is widespread in southern Europe and also grows in central Europe. It has medicinal properties and was formely used for both healing and cosmetics.

The dried leaves are used as seasoning — they are bitter and very aromatic. The flowering shoots and flowers are used by the cosmetic and pharmaceutical industries as a perfume.

Lavender is used as a spice in southern European cooking. Only a very little should be used, but it makes a good flavouring for roast meats, particularly when used with other herbs such as oregano, rosemary, hyssop, basil and thyme. It makes an excellent accompaniment to barbecued meat — a sprig can be added to the grilled meat. It also makes a good flavouring for cured meat and game.

Lavender leaves contain many essential oils (with linalool acetate), tannins (12 per cent), coumarin, bitter principles, resins and phytoncides. It eases spasms of the stomach and intestines, and regulates intestinal activity, and prevents diarrhoea. As a medicinal plant, lavender helps cure insomnia, heart palpitations and irritability and also helps reduce blood pressure.

It grows in southern, sunny regions in light, lime-rich soil. It is propagated by seeds or by the division of clumps in late summer. Old plants can be improved by pruning in late autumn. Basal cuttings, if covered with soil, will root. The leaves should be collected at the beginning of May and dried in the shade.

Garden Cress

Lepidium sativum L.

This is an annual plant of the family Cruciferae which grows up to 30cm (12in) high. The basal leaves are irregular, lyre-shaped and palmatisect, while the upper leaves on the stem are linear. It has white to pinkish flowers. The seeds are bright brown and shiny.

Garden Cress is native to northern Africa and western Asia. It is commonly cultivated in western Europe and America.

Only the fresh young leaves are used as a seasoning. They have a pleasant, pungent taste and distinctive scent, reminiscent of Mustard and Horseradish. The leaves are picked in the flowering period.

Cress is used for salads and as a flavouring for sandwiches. It is often used as a garnish on canapés, in cheese spreads, herbal butter and mayonnaise. It is also a useful garnish for meat and fish dishes.

Garden Cress is rich in vitamin C, and also contains carotene, vitamins B_1 and K, the glycoside of mustard oil, chlorophyll, iron and sulphur. It stimulates the metabolism, the secretion of gastric juices and bile. It is a diuretic and affects the formation of red corpuscles.

It can be grown in shallow bowls or boxes, either in humid cotton wool or sand. If provided with adequate warmth and light, it will sprout in two days and in a week reaches a height of about 5cm (2in) when it can be harvested. Garden Cress can also be grown in light sandy soil in pots, boxes or in garden beds. Under warm conditions, it grows fast and tolerates semi-shade.

Garden Salad

1 lettuce
225g (8oz) boiled potatoes
50g (2oz) boiled celery
50g (2oz) fresh cucumber
50g (2oz) radishes
25g (1oz) peppers (red or green)
100g (4oz) salami (or ham)

50g (2oz) garden cress
100 ml (1/4pint) mayonnaise
1 × 15ml spoon (1 tablespoon) onion
salt, pepper, lemon juice or vinegar to
   taste
hard boiled eggs for garnish

Wash and dry the lettuce and arrange the leaves on a plate. Chop all the other ingredients and mix with the mayonnaise and pile on top of the lettuce. Garnish with slices of hard boiled egg. Serve with brown bread and butter.

Serves 4

Lovage

Levisticum officinale Koch

Lovage is a stout perennial plant of the carrot family (Umbelliferae). The leaves are pinnate and a glossy dark green. It flowers from June to August and the pale yellow flowers are arranged in compound umbels. The fruits consist of yellow-brown achenes. The whole plant has an aroma similar to Celery. It is melliferous.

Lovage is native to western Asia. In southern Europe it is still found growing wild, although it has been cultivated in central Europe since the 12th century and was brought there from the Italian Liguria. Lovage is grown in gardens but it is also grown for industrial use and this has tended to reduce its cultivation elsewhere.

The fresh leaves are better for seasoning than the dried ones as they are more aromatic. They have a spicy taste which is sweetish to begin with and then has a bitter aftertaste. The roots and seeds are also used as a seasoning and both the roots and the young shoots have medicinal properties.

Lovage is used to flavour meat, vegetable and pulse soups. It is a frequent ingredient of mixed spice. Fresh Lovage is particularly good with tomato and pepper salads. Used finely chopped, it makes an excellent flavouring for stuffings, minced meat, and vegetable and meat stews. It can be used in cottage cheese spreads and in meat sauces. Just a few leaves are quite enough to flavour a whole dish. The seeds are used to flavour pickled vegetables, particularly mushrooms. Dried Lovage should be ground just before using and kept in a tightly closed jar away from the light.

Lovage contains mainly essential oils with terpineol. It also contains furocoumarins, vitamins, bitter principles, resin, sugars and organic acids. It stimulates the elimination of salt from the body and the secretion of digestive juices. It helps activate the bile and relieves flatulence.

Lovage is grown from seeds, pre-cultivated plants or by the division of adult plants. It is planted in spring, in deep, well-fertilized soil.

Marjoram
Majorana hortensis Moench, syn. *Origanum majorana* L.

This is an annual, biennial to perennial herb, up to 50cm (20in) high. The branched stems bear small, ovate leaves. The whole plant is fragrant, pale grey and woolly. The white and pink flowers form spikes in the axils of felted bracts. Marjoram is a representative of the family Labiatae. It flowers in July and its fruits are nutlets. The annual variety is preferred for cultivation.

Marjoram is probably indigenous to northern Africa. The Egyptians, Romans and Greeks used it mostly as a medicinal herb and it was a frequent ingredient of love potions. It is cultivated today mainly in central and southern Europe and in northern Africa and Egypt.

The dried leaves are used as a seasoning. Good-quality seasoning is a pale grey-green colour and very aromatic. Fresh Marjoram has a strong, distinctive, spicy scent and taste.

Marjoram is used often in central and southern European cuisine and also in North African dishes, but it is also frequently used in American and Asian cookery. It can be added to vegetable and pulse soups, to casseroles and stews (mainly mutton and beef). It goes well with fat poultry such as goose and duck, and is used in smoked products (sausages, salamis and pâtés, for example). It is used in stuffings, and with grilled meat.

Marjoram contains 2 to 3 per cent of essential oils, bitter principles, and almost 1 per cent of tannins. It stimulates digestion, has diuretic and anti-spasmodic effects and alleviates tension. It is recommended as a treatment for diarrhoea because of its high level of tannins, and is therefore a good addition to any fatty or indigestible food.

Marjoram may be grown in rock gardens as a perennial. It forms thick clumps with stems which run along the ground and themselves take root; it is hardy and grows easily. It can be cut several times a year and is propagated either by dividing the plants into clumps or by planting rooted stems. The annual variety can be cultivated in warm areas on a large scale. It can be grown either in gardens or pots, but it should always have a light, lime-rich soil. The leaves and stems are gathered whole, dried in the shade and shredded. Marjoram should be harvested before flowering and the leaves and stems cut to 5cm (2in) above the ground.

Fairy-ring Champignon

Marasmius oreades Bolton

This mushroom belongs to the family Tricholomataceae and is small and inconspicuous itself, but grows in large numbers. The stipe reaches 8cm (3in) in height and about 5mm (1/2in) in diameter. The cap is usually about 6cm (2in) in diameter and is pale ochre-yellow, as is the flesh. The gills are off-white and turn darker when damp. The whole mushroom has a pleasant scent and a mild, walnut-like taste.

It is usually found in the European temperate zone on pasture land or in lightly wooded areas. It grows in tufts and circles, from which springs the name 'fairy ring'. It can be easily cultivated and provides a good harvest.

For seasoning only the caps are used. It is delicious eaten either as a vegetable, in soups, or dried as a seasoning. Dried caps can be kept in a cool, dry place and used either whole or ground.

Marasmius scorodonius (Fries)

This mushroom should not be mistaken for an inedible type, *Micromphale perforans* (Fries, Singer), which has a thinner stalk and grows in colonies in spruce forests. The edible *Marasmius scorodonius* is smaller. It has a stalk of up to 6cm (2in) long and 2 to 5mm (1/5in) wide, paler in the upper part and darker below. The cap is 2 to 3cm (1in) wide, reddish brown, and white below and slightly conical. The gills are whitish to cream-coloured. The scent is strongly reminiscent of garlic.

It grows in the European temperate zone and can be found in large quantities near tree trunks and on grassy land after rainfall. For seasoning, the dry mushrooms may be used. They should be soaked before using to return them to their original size.

Top: *Marasmius oreades*
Bottom: *Marasmius scorodonius*

Lemon Balm

Melissa officinalis L.

This perennial plant grows up to 1m (3ft) high. It belongs to the family Labiatae and has a square, branched stem covered with numerous leaves in opposite arrangement. The leaves have rough serrate-dentate margins and a pronounced venation. The plant is softly hairy and netted with glands. The flowers grow in the axils of the leaves and are white, pinkish, pale blue or yellow-white. Lemon Balm flowers from June to August. It is a melliferous plant with a pleasant lemony scent and a spicy taste.

It originated from the eastern Mediterranean and is now established in southern Europe and south-western Asia. It was used by the Greeks and Romans as a medicament and seasoning and it still serves both purposes today. It used to be regarded as a cure for melancholy. Cultivated varieties of the plant are now grown all over the world, and it will grow wild in warmer climates.

The young leaves are collected before flowering and used as a seasoning. Dried Balm can also be used but it has less scent and is used mainly in mixed spices. Since the lemon scent evaporates fast, Balm should not be kept too long. It should be stored in tightly closed containers away from light.

Lemon Balm tastes best used fresh and is added, finely chopped, to prepared dishes. It can be used in anything which benefits from a lemony flavour but particularly in salads, soups, fish dishes, mayonnaises, milk and wine drinks, lemonades and vinegars. Rice can be improved with a few chopped leaves of fresh Balm.

The leaves contain a volatile oil, tannins, bitter principles and resins. Fresh Balm also contains vitamins and enzymes.

Lemon Balm improves the appetite, relieves flatulence and acts as a sedative. It soothes migraines and helps to reduce blood pressure.

Lemon Balm does well in sunny places in rich, clay soil. It can be sown directly in beds in April, or can be planted in seed trays and then planted out as seedlings. It can also be propagated by division of older clumps. It should be protected in the winter as it can easily be destroyed by frost. Lemon Balm can also be grown in pots and boxes. It should be harvested in dry, cool weather and dried in the shade.

Peppermint

Mentha piperita Hudson

A perennial cultivated plant of the family Labiatae, this is a multiple hybrid of several mint species. It forms shoots above and below the ground and the stems reach a height of about 80cm (32in). They bear opposite elliptical to lanceolate leaves and the pale scarlet flowers are arranged in dense spikes. The leaves are green to reddish, covered with glandular dots. The plant has a strong minty smell.

Mint was used as a seasoning by the Romans although it is not known which species was most common. It is now cultivated in a number of countries, principally in Europe and North America. Both the fresh and dried leaves and shoots can be used as a seasoning. The dry leaves should be green. If they are brown, it means that the drying process has not been done properly or that the leaves are damaged or diseased. Dried mint should have a strong minty smell and a spicy taste.

It is often mixed with other herbs to make a seasoning, and is particularly good in minced meat dishes and stuffings. It is also used to flavour cheeses, and fruit and vegetable salads. It aromatizes drinks, such as tea, and is suitable for sauces to go with roast meat such as lamb or mutton.

The leaves contain an essential oil (up to 2.5 per cent) with menthol, menthon, tannins (about 5 per cent), bitter principles, flavonoids and other components. Peppermint alleviates flatulence and affects the secretion of bile and soothes the stomach. Large doses and too frequent consumption of mint can be harmful.

Mint can only be propagated vegetatively and new plants are obtained by dividing old clumps either in spring or autumn. Alternatively, the underground shoots can be transplanted. Mint should be grown in humid, humus-rich soil in slightly shady conditions. It is harvested before flowering, several times a year, at mid-day. It dries fast in the shade at a temperature not exceeding 35°C (90°F).

Spearmint

Mentha crispa L.
Mentha spicata L.

Spearmint is a cultivated plant, a hybrid of several mint species. It is widely grown around the Balkans and Mediterranean.

The dried leaves and young shoots are used as a seasoning. They should be grey-green in colour with a spicy, cumin-like scent and a slightly astringent taste.

Spearmint is a common seasoning in the cuisine of Italy, France and the Balkans. It is used to flavour soups, particularly those made from pulses, and certain roast and grilled meat dishes popular in Balkan cooking.

It contains an essential oil (approximately 2.5 per cent, with carvone), tannins (6 per cent), bitter principles, and other constituents. It promotes the activity of the intestines, stomach and bile.

Stomma Kebab
(Bulgaria)

800g (1½lb) veal or lamb
4 × 15ml spoons (4 tablespoons) oil
2 large onions
3 × 15ml spoons (3 tablespoons) tomato purée
4 green peppers
1 × 15ml spoon (1 tablespoon) flour
1 × 15ml spoon (1 tablespoon) parsley
1 × 15ml spoon (1 tablespoon) fresh mint
1 × 5ml spoon (1 tablespoon) savory
1 × 5ml spoon (1 teaspoon) sweet pepper
1 chilli
salt
pepper
150ml (5oz) white wine

Cut meat into cubes and fry gently with the onions in half the oil. De-seed and slice the peppers into thin strips and add to pan. Add the spices, flour and salt and stir well. Add the wine and remaining oil, cook for a few minutes longer and then turn the mixture into a greased ovenproof dish. Cook at 160°C (325°F, Gas Mark 3) for about 1½ hours, or until tender.

Curry Leaf Tree
Murraya koenigii (L.) Sprengel

The Curry Leaf Tree belongs to the Rutaceae family. It is native to Ceylon and India, where it is grown for its aromatic, sharp-tasting leaves. Its name, in fact, derives from its use in curries and its leaves can be used fresh or dried. It is also reputed to be a tonic and a stomachic.

The leaves of the Curry Leaf Tree are used as a seasoning in curry which originated in eastern India; it is a finely ground mixture of various spices added to meat, fish, eggs, poultry and vegetables. The distinctive taste of the curry is derived from the proportions of spices mixed together and can vary from a very hot and peppery variety to a much milder, more aromatic kind.

The main ingredients of curry powder are chillies, turmeric, pepper, cumin, ginger, cardamom and coriander. The hotness will depend mainly on the amount of chilli powder used. The leaves of the Curry Leaf Tree are used to add extra piquancy to the curry.

The three recipes below are for a normal curry, a hot curry and a mild curry and represent the proportions of the spices to each other. The amount of the total mixture you use will depend on how strong you want the curry to be, and it is best to experiment to suit your taste.

Common curry	per cent	Hot curry	per cent	Mild curry	per cent
Turmeric	10	Cardamom	45	Cardamom	33
Chilli powder	7.5	Cloves	11	Clove	11.5
Ginger	7.5	Black pepper	14	Mace	5
Cinnamon	15	Nutmeg	3	Nutmeg	3
Cardamom	7.5	Mace	3	Turmeric	2.5
Black pepper	12.5	Cinnamon	10	Cumin	12
Coriander	30	Cumin	8	Cinnamon	30
Allspice	8	Chilli	3	Curry leaf	3
Curry leaf	2	Curry leaf	3		

Top: *Murraya koenigii*
Bottom: *Murraya paniculata*

Nutmeg

Myristica fragrans Houttuyn

The Nutmeg is an ornamental, tropical, evergreen tree of the family Myristiaceae. It grows to a height of about 8 to 16m (24 to 48ft). It has a dark green, conical crown and the trunk and branches are covered with smooth grey-green to olive coloured bark, which contains a liquid which turns red on contact with the air. The fruit is a one-seeded berry which is smooth on the surface and ochre-coloured with a reddish tint. It resembles a very tiny peach.

The Nutmeg tree is native to the Moluccas and is grown mainly in the islands of Banda, Amboina, Java, Borneo, Celebes and Sumatra. It is cultivated in other tropical regions but without much success.

The fruits have an inner part which forms the nutmeg and outer fleshy covering which yields the spice known as mace.

Both nutmeg and mace are used as a seasoning in white sauces, ragouts, soups, vegetables and meats. Nutmeg tends to be used more in sweeter dishes made from milk, such as custard and junket. Both are used in confectionery and perfumery, and for liqueurs.

Both nutmeg and mace contain an essential oil of which there is some 6 to 8 per cent in nutmeg and up to 17 per cent in mace. The essential oil yields the active principle myristicin, which gives it the distinctive fragrance and the pungent flavour. Nutmeg also contains 25 to 35 per cent oil with up to 12 per cent nutmeg acid. The oil is pressed from the nuts and is marketed as nutmeg butter, used both medicinally and in the perfume industry.

The fruits are hand-picked and gathered ripe. They are split and the outer layer is removed. The fleshy covering is then also removed, rolled out and dried. The seeds are also dried, the inner seed coverings removed, and the seeds themselves soaked in lime milk to prevent fungus forming.

Watercress

Nasturtium officinale R. Brown

Watercress is a perennial plant belonging to the family Cruciferae. It grows up to 80cm (32in) high and has a square, hollow stem with fleshy, odd-pinnate leaves. The white flowers have yellow anthers and are arranged in racemes. The fruits are sickle-shaped siliquas with two rows of seeds.

Watercress grows in temperate areas, preferably near water. The cultivated varieties are grown in Europe and the USA.

Watercress is used both as a seasoning and medicinally. The stalks and leaves can be collected in the spring and used in cooking, and the seeds are also occasionally used, in the same way as mustard seeds.

The leaves are most often used in salads or as a garnish for a variety of dishes, and the seeds are used to flavour stews. Watercress also makes a delicious, peppery-tasting soup.

The tops of the plants contain a glycoside which yields mustard oil, a high percentage of vitamin C and vitamins A and E. It stimulates the appetite and the activity of bile, and improves digestion. It also affects the activity of the pituitary gland. An excessive quantity of Watercress can irritate the urinary passages, however.

Chicken Sandwich Louis Armstrong
(USA)

Half a roast chicken, sliced
2 large thin slices bread
2 × 15ml spoons (2 tablespoons) shredded watercress
3 lettuce leaves
1 × 15ml spoon (1 tablespoon) mayonnaise
1 large slice ham or salami

1 × 15ml spoon (1 tablespoon) butter
3 radishes
3 or 4 rounds cucumber
2 × 15ml spoons (2 tablespoons) parsley
1 × 5ml spoon (1 teaspoon) mustard
salt
pepper
tomatoes for garnish

Butter bread and pile ingredients in layers on one buttered slice. Add salt and pepper, cover with remaining slice of bread and join with a toothpick. Garnish with sliced, seasoned tomatoes.

Love-in-a-mist

Nigella sativa L.

This is an annual plant of the family Ranunculaceae. It has finely divided leaves forming thread-like segments. The stem is erect, branched and approximately 60cm (24in) high. Love-in-a-mist flowers from June to September and the rough, tiny black seeds are ingrown in the fruit follicles. A more decorative variety, *Nigella damascena* L., is grown for its larger flowers which are star-shaped. The sepals are an off-white bluish colour with a green dot and green netting. The petals are shaped as two-lipped glands with stipes.

Love-in-a-mist is native to southern Europe and western Asia. In the warmer parts of central Europe it grows wild, but it is also cultivated, predominantly in southern Europe and in the Orient.

The seeds, which are sometimes also known as *damascene* or *black cumin,* are bitter and peppery. They smell a little like nutmeg and are used as a condiment in eastern Mediterranean and Oriental cuisine, and as a medicine in other places.

The seeds are used as a substitute for pepper, and to season bread. They can be added to any fatty dishes, and to most doughs and pastries.

The seeds contain a large quantity of oil, saponins (melanthin), essential oils (up to 1.5 per cent), tannins, the bitter principle nigellin and the alkaloid damascene. They have antispasmodic effects and stimulate the function of bile and intestinal activity. They are anthelmintic and influence lactation.

The seeds can replace pepper in small doses but not in large ones, as the melanthin can be toxic to warm-blooded creatures (and is, in fact, lethal to cold-blooded ones).

Basil

Ocimum basilicum L.

Basil is an annual herb, approximately 20 to 50cm (8 to 20in) tall, with a branched, reddish stem. The stalked leaves are oblong and ovate, with entire or crenate margins. Some varieties have crispated leaves of sundry colours — from pale green to red-purple — and of different sizes. Basil belongs to the family Lamiaceae. It flowers in odd whorls in August. The flowers are whitish to pale red. The herb is melliferous and has a clove-like scent. The fruits are blue-brown nutlets.

Basil is native to southern India and was brought to Europe in the 16th century from Iran and India. It is popular as a fragrant, decorative pot plant.

The leaves are usually used for seasoning but the flowering shoots can be used as well. Generally only the leaves are used fresh and the whole plant is dried. Good-quality dried Basil should be greenish or reddish in colour and when the leaves are pressed between the fingers they should give off a pleasant, strong aroma, rather like that of cloves or nutmeg.

As a seasoning, Basil can be used fresh in salads, on vegetables, in tomato sauces, on pasta and in pickled gherkins. Dried Basil can be added to stewed meat and vegetable dishes and to herbal butter.

Basil contains mainly essential oils (approximately 1.3 per cent) with methyl-chavicol and linalool, tannins, and organic acids. The fresh herb contains enzymes and mineral salts. It promotes gastric functions and improves the appetite as well as relieving flatulence and exerting an antispasmodic effect.

Basil requires loose, light soil, rich in humus, in a warm sunny place. It can be sown in hotbeds in March, and then transplanted when the plants reach about 8 to 10cm (3 to 4in) in height, in pairs in rows about 30cm apart. As a kitchen pot-herb it can be grown in boxes and pots, but should not be planted outside until the spring frosts are over. The leaves and shoots are collected at flowering time, but not all the leaves should be stripped off the plant. The cut shoots should be dried in the shade. Basil can be harvested two or three times between June and September.

Olive

Olea europaea L.

The Olive belongs to the family Oleaceae. The genus *Olea* comprises some 40 evergreen species which are indigenous to the tropical and sub-tropical regions. Only one species, *Olea europaea,* is cultivated for its fruit.

The Olive is cultivated in the Mediterranean region and the northern part of Asia Minor. It is also grown in North and South America, in south-western Africa and Australia. There are nearly 5 million hectares (about 12½ million acres) of olive plantations, 4 million of which are in Europe.

The fruit of the Olive is a spherical to oblong drupe, 1 to 4cm (1/2 to 1½in) long. Unripe olives are greyish green and when ripe the fruit changes colour, either to greenish-white, purple or black.

Only completely ripe fruit are used to make olive oil. The best grade, known as *Oleum virgineum,* is produced by mild pressure at a temperature of 20° to 25°C. It is then separated and refined, and is the purest type of oil. Two further grades can be made, *Oleum optimum* (from a second pressing), and a third grade, *Oleum commune,* from a third pressing. The latter type is only used industrially.

Olive fruits contain up to 40 per cent oil. Some varieties are grown just for their oil, while others are cultivated for the eating quality of their fruit.

Oregano (also known as Wild Marjoram)
Origanum vulgare L.

This is a perennial plant of the family Labiatae and is similar to, and related to, Marjoram. It has a branched, erect, reddish stem with ovate, opposite leaves. The purple flowers are arranged in heads and appear in July and August. It is melliferous and has a pleasant smell.

Oregano is found throughout Europe and Asia and also in America. It grows on sunny slopes, in lightly wooded areas. It has a long tradition of use as a spice and as a medicinal herb. It was even once regarded as being magical — protecting people and cattle against disease — and it was also used as a love potion.

For seasoning, the stalks and leaves are used (usually dried). The dried leaves are a greyish-green. Oregano has a distinctive spicy scent and a slightly bitter taste.

Oregano is used in stews and soups. As it has a strong flavour, only a little should be used.

Oregano contains an essential oil with thymol as the main constituent, some 8 per cent tannins, bitter principles and other substances. It is renowned for improving the appetite and increasing the secretion of the bile. Its high content of tannins helps prevent diarrhoea.

It can be propagated from seed, sown in a sunny place in the garden, or by division of clumps of the plant. It can be picked wild as well. June is the best time for harvesting the plant: only the fleshy parts of the stem and the leaves are gathered, before noon, and then dried at a temperature of up to 35°C.

Jambalaya
(Mexico)

500g (1lb) smoked meat (such as frankfurters)
250g (8oz) rice
1 large onion
1 clove garlic
400g (14oz) tomatoes
1 chilli

2 green peppers, de-seeded
salt
black pepper
1 × 5ml spoon (1 teaspoon) paprika
1 × 5ml spoon (1 teaspoon) oregano
3 × 15ml spoons (3 tablespoons) oil

Chop the onion and crush the garlic and fry in 2 × 15ml spoons (2 tablespoons) of oil. Add the peppers, sliced thinly, the tomatoes cut in quarters and the chopped chilli. Cook gently until soft. Meanwhile, boil the rice until tender. Cut the meat into small cubes and fry in 1 × 15ml spoon (1 tablespoon) of oil. Add seasonings and cook until heated thoroughly. Then mix with the vegetables and pour over the drained rice. Leave in a warm oven for 10 minutes before eating.

Opium Poppy

Papaver somniferum L.

This annual plant of the family Papaveraceae reaches a height of 1m (3ft). The stem and lobed leaves are bluish and usually glabrous. The plant is interwoven with latex canals and the flower stalks are crooked. Poppies have hanging buds which straighten up when they begin to blossom. The calyx is deciduous with a corolla composed of four petals, white, pink, red or purple with brown purple patches. The ovary, which is barrel-shaped and covered by a star-like stigma, produces the fruit − a capsule with partitions. The ripe seeds are blue-black or white, pink, brown or grey-blue.

The poppy originated in the Near East and it has since become common in central Europe. It dates back to ancient times and is used both medicinally and in cooking. The ripe seeds, used as a seasoning, should have a spicy, sweetish taste.

Poppy seeds have a number of uses in cooking. They can be used as a sweet filling in pastry, or as substitute for nuts. Whole seeds are often used for decoration on bread and cakes. Poppy seeds are also an ingredient of mixed spices, particularly in the Orient, where they are added to curry mixtures.

The ripe poppy seed contains approximately 30 per cent oil. The more dangerous alkaloids are found in the capsules and unripe seeds and serve as the raw material for the production of drugs such as opium (although this is not found in the European varieties). Poppy seed has a high nutritive value − it contains a lot of mineral substances, proteins, glycides, organic acids, etc. Poppy seed stimulates the appetite.

Poppies are not generally cultivated in gardens but they grow easily in loamy soil, rich in humus. The seeds should be sown in early spring, in rows about 30cm (12in) apart. They need regular fertilizing and watering.

Parsnip

Pastinaca sativa L.

This biennial plant of the family Umbelliferae reaches a height of 40 to 100cm (16 to 40in). The stalk is branched in the upper part and is square and furrowed. The whole plant is hairless or covered with thin, coarse hairs. The leaves, which are often glossy, are pinnate with 3 to 7 leaflets on the sides and one at the tip. The Parsnip flowers from June to August with the flowers formed in 5 to 20 paired umbels in a ray-like arrangement, usually without scales. The small flowers have bright yellow petals. The fruit, achenes, reach a length of 5 to 7cm (2 to 3in) and are ovate and flat with a narrow, flattened, yellow-brown outgrowth.

The parsnip is native to Eurasia and is both cultivated and exists in the wild. It is now also found in America as a common weed. It usually grows in the wild in damp meadows and along roadsides and embankments.

Only cultivated Parsnips can be used for cooking. Wild Parsnip is too woody and bitter. Cultivated Parsnip roots are either used as a vegetable, in the same way as carrots, or the oils in the roots can be used to produce mixed spices and condiments. The grated root is sometimes used as a substitute for coffee but the taste is not to everyone's liking.

The plant contains a high quantity of furocoumarins, and the fruit also yields oils and calcium-oxalate. The roots and fruit were once used to make medicines to relieve toothache, to lower fever and as a cure for tuberculosis. The roots have a higher nutritional value than the carrot.

Parsnips can be grown in heavy soil which should be dug deeply and thoroughly, and broken up to allow to develop without forked roots developing. The seed is sown in autumn or early spring with enough space between seeds and rows to allow the roots room to grow. The roots can be harvested 6 months after sowing, but as they are frost-resistant they can be left in the ground and used when needed.

Parsnips aux Fines Herbes
(France)

750g (1½lb) parsnips
60g (2oz) butter
1 × 15ml spoon (1 teaspoon) each of
  fresh chives, parsley, basil and marjoram
ground black pepper
salt
Wash, peel and cut parsnips into 3cm (1½in) cubes. Cook until tender in salted water.
Toss in butter with herbs. Add salt and pepper to taste. Serve with grilled or roast
meat dishes.

Serves 4

Parsley

Petroselinum hortense Hoffman,
syn. *Petroselinum crispum* (Miller) A. W. Hill

Parsley is a well-known biennial-to-perennial garden plant, forming its leaves and a thickened tapering root in the first year's growth, and stems with greenish-yellow, umbellate flowers and fruits in the following year. The fruit are small, green-brown achenes. There are many improved varieties grown as root vegetables, while others are bred simply for the leaves, such as Crispate Parsley *(P. hortense* var. *crispum)*.

Parsley is native to the Mediterranean and has a long history dating back to the 3rd century AD. It was used then as a seasoning. Charles the Great introduced it to Europe and its use as a seasoning and medicinal herb then spread all over the world.

The fresh leaves of any of the varieties of Parsley can be used for seasoning. The seeds, roots and stalks are also used, dried and ground, as an ingredient of mixed herbs. The dried leaves can also be used for seasoning.

Parsley can be added to most dishes, but particularly to stuffings, sauces and egg dishes. It makes a decorative garnish for fish, cold meat, salads and canapés, and is used in soups and casseroles.

Fresh Parsley leaves are rich in vitamin C and also contain carotene. The root contains a smaller quantity of vitamin C, and vitamins B_1, B_2 and PP. The whole plant is rich in essential oil (apiol oil is the main constituent) but most is found in the fruit and leaves. The leaves are also rich in magnesium and iron. In small quantities, Parsley root, leaves and fruit improve the appetite, help digestion and increase the secretion of urine. Sufferers from kidney inflammation and pregnant women should not eat too much parsley.

Parsley grows in quite poor soil. It should be sown from April to July, and usually takes at least 3 weeks to sprout. To keep fresh parsley throughout the winter, plant some in pots on a sunny window-sill. It can also be grown from root pieces, which, if kept just covered with water, rapidly send out shoots.

Centre: *Pastinaca sativa*
Left and right: *Petroselinum hortense*

Allspice Tree (also known as **Pimento**)

Pimenta dioica (L.) Merrill, syn. *Pimenta officinalis* Lindley

This is a robust, evergreen tree of the family Myrtaceae. It reaches a height of 10 to 20m (30 to 60ft) and has a widely branched crown and the trunk is covered with pale, smooth, aromatic bark. The leaves are glossy and leathery, and have a pleasant smell. The fruits are spherical, pea-sized berries with a persistent remainder of the calyx at the top. Unripe berries are green and turn scarlet when ripe.

Allspice is indigenous to Central America, Mexico and Jamaica. It did not reach Europe until the 17th century when, owing to its great popularity in England, it was also known as 'English spice', although it has also been called 'Jamaican pepper'. The name allspice derives from the blend of spice flavours contained in the one plant. The small fruits are harvested while still green and are hand-picked and dried in the sun or in drying kilns. Well-dried fruit are graded according to size.

Allspice flavours smoked products, canned meats and sauces, soups, fish marinades and game. It is an important ingredient in a number of mixed spices, either whole or ground. It was also used by natives of Central America to flavour chocolate.

The active principle of this spice is the essential oil − pimento oil − which gives it its spicy, pungent taste. The leaves and fruit are distilled for this oil (they contain some 3 to 4 per cent) which is used as an aromatizing essence in the manufacture of liqueurs, perfumery and medicine.

Anise

Pimpinella anisum L.

This is an annual plant of the carrot family, Umbelliferae. It grows to a height of about 50cm (20in). The stem, which is erect, hollow and noded, grows from a tap root. The basal leaves are simple and undivided, the central leaves are foliate and the upper ones are sessile, sheathed, filiform and lanceolate. Anise flowers from June to August; its white flowers are arranged in cymes. The fruit is a pear-shaped achene, 2 to 5mm (1/4 to 1/2in) long. All parts of the plant are aromatic.

Anise has been known since 1500 BC. It was praised by the Egyptians and ancient Romans, and has never lost its reputation as a medicament and seasoning.

The plant is native to the Mediterranean and Asia Minor. It is cultivated in Spain, Italy, Bulgaria, the USSR, France, Turkey, Cyprus, India, Mexico, and Czechoslovakia.

The fruits — aniseed (the seed of Anise) — are used as a condiment. They should be yellow to grey-green, with an aromatic, spicy smell. Brown aniseed is stale. It should be stored in dark, tightly closed containers.

As a seasoning aniseed is added to pastry, biscuits and bread. It can also be added to pickles, liqueurs and to sweets. It can be used in curry mixtures and is popular in both Indian and Chinese cuisine to flavour meat dishes.

The fruit contains a fragrant volatile oil (up to 6 per cent) with anethol. It also contains oil, mucilages, proteins, glycides, cholin and other substances. Anise has a strong antispasmodic effect, even more so than Cumin or Fennel.

Anise should be grown in sunny, wind-sheltered locations on warm, light, clay-sandy soil rich in lime. Seeds are sown in March or April in rows about 15 to 35cm (6 to 14in) apart. It is not usually grown in gardens.

Burnet Saxifrage

Pimpinella saxifraga L.

This is a perennial plant of the family Umbelliferae. The thickened, tapering root sends out odd-pinnate basal leaves with unevenly dentate leaflets. The grooved stem grows from a basal rosette of leaves. It reaches a height of up to 50cm (20in) with a compound umbel of small flowers (white, yellowish or pinkish). It flowers from June till the autumn and grows in dry meadows, on hillsides and embankments and in light woods and shrubberies in Europe and western Asia.

It can be found in both lowland and mountainous regions and was once believed to protect men from the plague.

The fresh leaves are used as a seasoning, and the root is used as a medicinal drug, although it was once used to flavour beer. Burnet leaves have a spicy, sweetish, slightly sharp taste with a mild cucumber-like aftertaste.

The leaves can be added to soups, sauces and salads, and to flavour mayonnaise, herbal butter and cheese spreads. A green sauce (also known as *salsa verde*) can be made with Burnet Saxifrage, combined with hard-boiled eggs, fully chopped, and French dressing. Other chopped herbs, such as parsley, sorrel, tarragon, chervil, cress and fennel leaves should be added. The sauce is usually served with grilled meat and fish, or boiled vegetables.

The leaves are collected in the wild in the spring before the stem grows from the basal rosette. The plant can be grown in gardens or in boxes and does well in rockeries, in dry sunny places. It is easy to grow, and very hardy.

The leaves of Burnet Saxifrage contain essential oils, coumarin, furocoumarin, pimpinellin, tannins, saponins and vitamins; they regulate the metabolism and soothe digestive disorders as well as stimulating the appetite.

Indian Long Pepper

Piper longum L.

Cubeb Pepper

Piper cubeba L.

Betel

Piper betle L.

In addition to the important seasoning provided by the pungent berries of Black Pepper *(Piper nigrum),* there are many other species of the genus *Piper.*

One of these is Indian Long Pepper, which has similar external characteristics to Black Pepper, but differs in its berries, which are arranged in a spike and grow together to form a catkin approximately 5cm (2¹/₂in) long, 5 to 8mm (1/5 – 1/3in) thick, grey-brown to black-brown. Unripe spikes are collected and used as a seasoning, mainly in Indonesia. Its smell is less intense than that of Black Pepper, but the taste is very sharp and peppery. The species *Piper officinarum* – Javanese Long Pepper – has the same appearance, use and distribution.

Another species, Cubeb Pepper *(Piper cubeba),* has much longer and narrower leaves than the Javanese species; the leaves are obliquely deltoid below. The fruits are brown-black, wrinkled berries, slightly larger than those of Black Pepper. They are arranged in dense, cylindrical clusters and elongated into characteristic stalks. For this reason, it is sometimes called 'Tailed Pepper'. It is grown mainly in the islands of Java and Sumatra. Instead of the active principle piperin, present in the other species, it contains the pungent cubebin, and an essential oil and resin. It also yields the so-called 'cubeb camphor'. Cubeb Pepper is used in folk medicine.

Guinean or Ashanti Pepper *(Piper guineense)* is found in central Africa. It also has long-stalked berries like Cubeb Pepper. Its active principle is piperin. The aborigines use it as a seasoning.

The Betel *(Piper betle)* is not used as a condiment, but its sharp-tasting juicy leaves with their tea-like aroma are chewed together with Areca nuts *(Areca catechu);* a grain of unslaked lime is also added to a Betel roll. The chewing of Betel leaves is a common habit in the Orient: Betel is one of the best-known and oldest narcotic drugs. *Piper methysticum* is used for similar purposes: in south-eastern Asia, it is made into a stupefying drink called 'kawa-kawa'.

South America and Cuba are the home of *Piper angustifolium;* its small black berries are used as a seasoning, and the foliage, 'matico', as a healing agent for stopping haemorrhages.

Top left: *Piper longum*
Top right: *Piper cubeba*
Bottom: *Piper betle*

Black Pepper

Piper nigrum L.

Black or True Pepper is a climbing tropical plant with a woody base. It belongs to the family Piperaceae. The shrub reaches 6 to 7m (20 to 23ft) in height, and the trunk is knotted, elastic, with aerial roots. The leaves are petiolate, broadly oblong and ovate, cordate towards the base. The spikes of Black Pepper are 8 to 10cm (3 to 4in) long and pendent. The fruit is a berry with a thin pulpous layer, green in the early stage, red or yellow-red later. Each spike contains 20 to 30 pea-sized berries. The plant flowers three times a year.

It is native to the Malabar coast of eastern India; its cultivation is most widespread in the Asiatic tropics.

It is propagated vegetatively by hardwood cuttings. The life expectancy of a plantation can be 25 to 30 years. Black Pepper does best near the sea, in humid soil rich in humus.

The first harvest usually takes place the third year after planting. The berries are usually gathered twice a year. The time of the harvest depends on the sort of seasoning to be obtained: Black or White Pepper. Black Pepper comes from unripe berries, which are picked immediately, when the lower-situated berries in the spike begin to redden. The collected berries are spread out in the sun and dried. They can also be soaked in boiling water and dried rapidly in drying kilns. Black Pepper berries are wrinkled and brown-black to black. Unripe berries are sometimes pickled in vinegar or in a salt solution: these are called 'Green Pepper' and praised by gourmets.

White Pepper is obtained from the same plants, but the berries are harvested after they have ripened, when the outer, pulpous layer can easily be separated from the white centre. Following a soaking and a brief fermentation, the outer layer is removed, the white seed is dried, and the final colour is yellow-grey. The taste and aroma of White Pepper is much more delicate than that of Black Pepper.

Pepper contains a pungent resin, essential oil and the alkaloid piperin, irritating the mucous membrane and promoting digestion. Pepper is also a source of phytoncides, and in moderate doses can favourably stimulate the stomach lining; it probably also stimulates slightly the activity of the heart. It is a diuretic and improves the metabolism. It is, however, an irritant and very large doses can be harmful.

Pepper, either whole in berries, ground, or in mixtures, is one of the most popular culinary condiments. It flavours meat, soups, sauces and salads, and smoked and canned products.

Portulaca (also known as **Purslane**)

Portulaca oleracea L. ssp. *sativa* (Haworth) Čelakowsky

This is a low-growing plant, 15 to 30cm (6 to 12in) high, with fleshy, oval, green leaves and a thick, rounded, pulpy, reddish-tinted stem. The pale yellow, star-like flowers grow from leaf axils and at the top of the plant. Ornamental forms have larger flowers, white to rich red in colour.

Portulaca is native to India where it grows wild. It has spread to the warmer regions of central Europe, and it now grows wild there too. It has medicinal properties and is also used in cooking. Only the fresh, young, fleshy leaves are used, gathered before the flowering period. They have a fresh, spicy, slightly salty taste.

Portulaca can be made into a green salad on its own, with a vinaigrette dressing, or it can be added to other salads. It makes a good flavouring for soups and sauces, but in all cooked dishes should be added in the last few minutes of cooking time. It can be used as a flavouring for mayonnaise, to make herbal butter, and chopped up finely as a garnish for tomato salads.

The plant contains many vitamins (A and C), mineral substances, glycides and proteins. It has diuretic properties and stimulates the appetite. The mineral substances prevent excessive acidity in the stomach. It makes a useful 'pick-me-up' in the spring, after a long winter.

It can be grown by sowing directly into the soil, either in garden beds or boxes. It should be sown in April in a light garden soil in a sunny place. It grows fast and the first leaves can be picked within a month. They should be harvested before the flowering stage, otherwise they will be too tough.

Pomegranate

Punica granatum L.

The Pomegranate is a sub-tropical, deciduous, densely-branched shrub or tree reaching a height of about 5m (15ft). Older branches of the tree are usually thorny. The flowers appear either individually or in small bunches, and have short stalks. The flowers are usually glossy red, but occasionally they can be yellow or white. They are bisexual and have no scent. The fruit is a large, spherical berry, either red, yellow, greenish or white (and very occasionally deep purple), with a persistent calyx. It weighs betwen 200 and 800g (7oz to 1½lbs). The skin of the berry is hard and leathery, about 2 to 3cm (3/4 to 1¼in) thick. The fruits contain seeds coated in a gelatinous pulp, and are rich in juice. The seeds and the pulp are red, pink or yellow-white.

The Pomegranate is probably native to Iran, Afghanistan and some parts of southern Arabia. Varieties bearing large fruit are cultivated in the Mediterranean and in Soviet Central Asia. Pomegranates are also grown in dry sub-tropical regions – in Africa, California, Louisiana, Florida and some parts of South America.

The credit for bringing Pomegranates to the Mediterranean is generally attributed to the Phoenicians: the name *Punica,* in fact, is related to the Roman name for Carthage *(poeni).*

The fruit of the Pomegranate is usually eaten raw, but is sometimes processed to make a grenadine syrup, and added to various sherbets, other syrups and wines.

The rind of the Pomegranate is rich in tannins, and is used medicinally and to cure leather. The leaves are dried to make tea, and the roots and rind processed to make black dye.

Sicilian Sumac (also known as **Tanner's Sumac**)
Rhus coriaria L.

This is a robust shrub of the family Anacardiaceae. It has resinous canals and tannin sacs in the bast and bark, and yellow, felted twigs. Its hairy, pinnate leaves are composed of 11 to 15 leaflets arranged on a flattened tapering stalk. The flowers form thyrsoid panicles and are bisexual. The fruit forms a panicle of drupes wrapped in a red-coloured, hairy, sour coating.

Sumac is found from the Canary Islands to Iran. It is also grown in the Mediterranean and around the Caucasian mountains. According to some sources, Sumac was once used by the Eastern nations instead of salt.

The dried, crushed drupes provide a condiment which forms a reddish powder with an astringent, sour taste. It can be used to replace lemon pulp. The dried drupes were also once used as a medicament, and to make red dye, and the wood and leaves were used in tanneries to provide a yellowish dye for the hides.

Sumac is used in cooking as a seasoning for barbecued meat, and for various meat and vegetable casseroles, particularly of chicken.

The fruit of the Sumac contains organic acids, pigments, resins and many tannins. It is recommended with fatty dishes since it prevents diarrhoea and helps the digestion.

Shashlik
(Armenia)

1kg (2lb) mutton (or pork)	quartered tomatoes for garnish
2 onions	2 × 15ml spoons (2 tablespoons) tarragon
2 × 15ml spoons (2 tablespoons) oil	(or basil or coriander)
2 × 15ml spoons (2 tablespoons)	salt
sumac	pepper

Cut the meat into bite-sized pieces and season with salt and pepper. Sprinkle with the herbs. Slice the onions. Thread the meat and slices of onion alternately on skewers and leave in the refrigerator for 4 to 6 hours. Baste with oil or bacon rind and barbecue or grill. Serve garnished with tomato slices and salad.

Rose

Rosa sp.

The ancestors of modern roses are erect or climbing thorny shrubs with odd-pinnate leaves. The flowers have five petals and form an aggregate fruit of achenes called a hip. Roses are found over the whole of the northern hemisphere. There are many varieties. The common Dog Rose *(Rosa canina)* is found in the wild. Its hips and petals (which are white to deep pink) are used for seasoning. The Damask Rose *(Rosa damascena)* has leaves which are glossy above and hairy on the underside. It has small pink or white flowers arranged in corymbs. A full flowered variety is known as *R.d. trigintipetala* and comes from Syria. It has red flowers which are distilled into attar of roses and rose water. Both hips and flowers are used for culinary purposes.

Hips, usually crushed into paste or dried, are used in game sauces and ragouts. They are also crushed and turned into a syrup.

The hips are normally picked in September or October. They contain up to 3 per cent vitamin C, carotene, vitamin B, tannins, citric and malic acids, sugar and mucilages. They stimulate the appetite, act as a diuretic and tonic and prevent capillary haemorrhages.

Rosemary

Rosmarinus officinalis L.

Rosemary is an evergreen shrub of the family Labiatae, approximately 1m (3ft) high. It has linear, leathery leaves, which are dark green above and off-white below. The flowers are pale purple to pale blue and grow from the leaf axils. The plant has a pleasant, camphor-like smell and flowers from May to August.

Rosemary is native to the Mediterranean region, where it is commonly found, but it also grows around the Black Sea. It is often grown as a house plant in central Europe because of its sensitivity to frost. In ancient times it was well known as a medicinal plant and a condiment.

The fresh or dried leaves can be used as a seasoning, whole, crushed, or ground. Gathered from June to August, they are dried in the shade at a temperature not exceeding 40°C.

Rosemary is widely used in European and American cuisine. It has a pungent aroma and so only a little need be used as a flavouring. It makes an excellent addition to all grilled or roasted fish, meat and poultry, to smoked products, soups, potatoes and pasta. It is a common ingredient of mixed herbs, particularly in the Mediterranean region.

Rosemary contains a number of essential oils (up to 2 per cent with cineol, horneol, etc.), tannins (8 per cent), phytoncides, bitter principles, saponins and resins. In small doses, it stimulates the flow of gastric juices and bile, and improves the appetite. It also reduces spasms of the smooth muscle and intestines; it limits the growth of bacteria and strengthens the nervous system. It is banned in pregnancy even as a seasoning.

Rosemary is cultivated from cuttings, usually about 10 to 20cm (4 to 8in) long. The shoots are cut off and rooted in damp garden soil or sand in spring or early summer. Because of its sensitivity to frost, it should be grown indoors in colder regions. It can be grown from seed and must not be over-watered.

Rue

Ruta graveolens L., ssp. *hortensis* Miller

Rue, a member of the family Rutaceae, is a perennial herb, a semi-shrub reaching 100cm (40in) in height. It has a branched, partly woody axis. The leaves are yellow green, palmatisect and thick. Against the light, oily dots can be seen in them. Rue has tiny yellow flowers arranged in cymes. It flowers from June to September and the fruits are multi-seeded capsules with black-grey seeds. It is a melliferous plant.

Rue was used as a seasoning by the ancient Romans. It used to be commonly cultivated, along with sage, in central Europe, and is native to the Mediterranean region.

The young leaves, either fresh or dried, are used for culinary purposes. The dried leaves are sometimes used in powdered form. They are pale yellow-green and have a faint bitter taste and a strong, distinctive smell when fresh.

Fresh Rue is used in cooking to flavour salads and sauces and to make herbal butter. Used with Sage, it makes an excellent flavouring for mutton, and, used in conjuction with Thyme, Bay leaves and Juniper, it is good with game. Fresh Rue should be added to food just before the end of the cooking time, and only a little used – one 5ml spoonful (one teaspoonful) per 500g (1lb) of food is quite enough.

Rue contains an essential oil, the glycoside rutin, tannins and bitter principles, and photosensitizing furocoumarins which provoke skin allergies in people susceptible to them. The glycoside rutin helps strengthen the capillaries. Rue stimulates the appetite, improves digestion and has a mild diuretic effect. It can be harmful in large doses. A fresh rue leaf on a piece of buttered bread clears the breath of the smell of garlic. It is generally prohibited during pregnancy as it increases the blood flow to the smooth muscle.

Garden Sage

Salvia officinalis L.

Sage is a perennial semi-shrub reaching about 1m (3ft) in height. It belongs to the family Labiatae. The stems and young leaves are felted, slightly wrinkled and grey-green or silvery green. The blue-purple or pinkish flowers, appearing in June and July, grow in a sparse inflorescence.

Sage is native to the Mediterranean and is most widespread in southern France, Greece, Dalmatia and Italy. It was used as a seasoning in ancient Rome and recipes contained in the work of Apicius Caelius are still used today in Italian cuisine. Sage is grown throughout central Europe.

The young leaves and plant tops are used in cooking, usually in dried form. Well-dried leaves should have a greenish-grey or silver-grey colour and a good, strong aroma. Sage tastes spicy and astringent with a predominant tannin tartness, and it is highly aromatic.

Sage is used in southern Europe either mixed with other herbs or to flavour goulash or barbecued meat. It makes a suitable seasoning for mutton, lamb and veal and for fish (particularly for eel). It goes well with minced meat and offal and is used for stuffing roast meat, particularly pork and goose. It also goes well with pasta and is used in herbal butter, blended with Parsley, Mint and Hyssop. Mixed with Mint, Rosemary, Savory, Marjoram, Oregano and Basil, Sage makes an excellent flavouring for hamburgers. Never use it in large quantities – one Sage leaf (or small pinch of dried Sage) is enough for one portion of meat.

Another species, Clary Salvia *(Salvia sclarea)*, is sometimes used for seasoning. It has a musky scent, rather reminiscent of Lavender.

Sage leaves contain essential oils (up to 2.5 per cent) with the main components thujone, saviol and cineol; a high percentage of tannin (more than 10 per cent), hormones, bitter principles, resins, and an amide of nicotinic acid. It improves the digestion and the activity of bile and the liver. It has anti-inflammatory properties and restricts the growth of bacteria. It is reputed to inhibit sweating and can be used as a gargle.

Sage is best grown in dry, lime-rich soil with sufficient sunlight. It is propagated from seeds sown in the spring, or by division of clumps of the existing plant. It can be grown in gardens, in rockeries, perennial beds or pots. It is harvested twice a year and the leaves should be collected before the flowering stage, at noon in dry weather. In spring the plants should be cut back to some 15cm (6in) above the ground to help the new foliage to form. The leaves should be dried in the shade and the drying finished at a temperature up to 35°C (90°F).

Summer Savory

Satureja hortensis L.

Mountain Savory
(also known as **Winter Savory**)

Satureja montana L.

Savory is an annual herb of the family Labiatae. It is a low-growing plant, reaching about 20 to 30cm (8 to 12in) in height with a woody, shrub-like stem and aromatic, narrow, linear leaves dotted with glands. Savory has small white or pink-purple flowers which appear from June to September. The fruits are mericarpia. There is another species, a perennial, called Mountain or Winter Savory which grows wild in parts of southern Europe.

Savory is native to the Mediterranean, and can also be found on the southern slopes of the Caucasus. It was used in Roman cuisine and reached central Europe in the ninth century. It has since become widely cultivated in most parts of Europe and North America.

Both the tops and leaves of Savory, either fresh or dried, can be used as a seasoning, but the young tops have the best flavour. Savory should be bright green, with a pleasant scent and a spicy, peppery taste. It makes a good substitute for pepper.

Savory can be used in all meat dishes which are normally seasoned with pepper. It blends well with cabbage, either on its own or with Thyme, and is good as a flavouring for pulses. It can be used as a seasoning in salads, with game and in cream sauces, many sorts of vegetable dishes, particularly with tomato soups and sauces. Only a small amount of Savory is needed — one stem or one 5ml spoon (a teaspoonful) of crushed Savory for a dish for four people, added at the last moment of cooking.

Savory can be used to flavour grilled chicken pieces. Use fresh, chopped Savory and coat the chicken a couple of hours before cooking. Sprinkle with a little salt, curry powder or ginger, and grill the chicken in the usual way.

Savory contains an essential oil and tannins. It is not just a tasty seasoning, but is used medicinally — it helps cure diarrhoea and has an anti-inflammatory and carminative effect.

Savory grows well in warm, sunny places in good garden soil. It can be grown in pots or boxes or in the garden. It sprouts in two weeks and is sown in shallow rows 20cm (8in) apart. Harvesting is done before flowering in June or July. Drying should be done quickly at a temperature of up to 35°C (90°F). Mountain Savory can be grown in rock-gardens and is even more decorative, with tougher, dark green leaves.

Sesame

Sesamum indicum L.

The genus *Sesamum* includes some 20 species and many varieties. The species *Sesamum indicum* is the most common.

It is possible that Sesame was introduced to India and China from Africa but it is now extensively cultivated in both areas, as well as in other tropical and sub-tropical regions. The main exporters of Sesame are India, South America, Japan, parts of Africa, Egypt, and the Near East and Central Asia.

Sesame seeds are pressed to produce excellent oil. The oil is pale yellow and odourless and is used in cooking and in the manufacture of sweets, margarines, in the cosmetic industry and medicinally. The husks from the pressed seeds are also used, as they are nourishing and easily digestible. These are used for sweets, bread, pastries and sauces, and also as animal fodder.

The whole seeds may be sprinkled on pastry or bread, and are ground into various oriental sweets, particularly Turkish delight or halva, which is made of ground sesame, lemon, honey, whipped egg whites and citric or tartaric acid.

The flowers are used pressed for perfume and toilet water.

Rowan (also known as **Mountain Ash**)

Sorbus sp.

The Rowan or Mountain Ash is a tree belonging to the family Rosaceae. It is a slender tree approximately 20 m (60ft) high with a sparse conical or oval crown, odd-pinnate leaves with 9 to 17 lanceolate, toothed leaflets (the dentation covers half the length of the leaflet). The flowers are small, pentamerous, arranged in a corymbose panicle. The fruits are glossy, scarlet pomes with yellow dots (known colloquially as berries) and they have a sweet-sour taste.

The Rowan is widespread in Europe and Asia and can be found in quite mountainous regions and also quite far north. It is native to the Mediterranean and was known to the Romans who used the berries both for seasoning and medicinally.

In culinary use, Rowan berries are pressed into juice, made into jam, or preserved. They make an excellent sauce for game or as a garnish to fat roast meat and other rich dishes.

The fruit is rich in vitamin C, contains a large amount of carotene, some 14 per cent of glycides (sorbit), many organic acids, the sorbic and parasorbic acids, malic acid, tannins, bitter principles and pectin, as well as other constituents.

Top left: *Sorbus terminalis*
Top right: *Sorbus aucuparia*
Bottom left: *Sorbus aria*
Bottom right: *Sorbus domestica*

Clove

Syzygium aromaticum (L.) Merrill,
syn. *Eugenia caryophyllata* Thunberg

This is an evergreen tropical tree which grows up to 10m (30ft) high, belonging to the family Myrtaceae. The forked trunk has many lateral branches covered with smooth, grey bark. The leaves are leathery, glossy, and dark green above and paler below, with numerous oil glands in the form of dots. The crushed leaves are highly aromatic.

The Clove is native to the Molucca Islands, but is cultivated widely in the Indo-Malayan region, off the East African coast in Madagascar, Reunion and Mauritius, as well as in the West Indies. The latter islands now supply the world with four-fifths of the total market. The best-quality cloves, however, come from the Molucca Islands and this species is known as the 'Royal Clove'. Cloves have been used as a seasoning since time immemorial. The first records date from China, in the third century BC, when they were used by the Chinese both to cure toothache and sweeten the breath. The Romans also used cloves and they were introduced to Europe in the Middle Ages.

The part of the Clove used as a seasoning is the unopened flower bud, but the dried ripe fruits are also used as a seasoning, or preserved in sugar. Clove is used whole as a spice and also in the manufacture of smoked food and liqueurs, in perfumery and in pharmaceutics. It can also be used ground or pressed to produce a nearly colourless liquid, oil of cloves, used as an antiseptic and in toothpastes.

The cups of the Clove buds contain a high percentage of volatile oil (14 to 21 per cent) with a substance called eugenol representing the basic active component. It improves the appetite and regulates the digestion.

Alecost (also known as Costmary)

Balsamita mayor Desfontaines,
syn. *Tanacetum balsamita* L.,
Chrysanthemum balsamita (L.)

This species belongs to the family Compositae. It is a perennial, tall, very aromatic herb with a creeping rhizome. It has an erect, robust and richly branched stem. The large, leathery, undivided, elliptical leaves have finely serrated margins. The tiny flowerheads grow at the ends of branches in dense corymbs.

The plant was introduced into Europe in the 16th century from China; it is native to western Asia but has subsequently been grown in Europe as a medicinal and aromatic plant, and now also grows wild.

The leaves of Alecost are used both medicinally and for culinary purposes. They have a pleasant scent, reminiscent of menthol, Lemon, Balm and Sage. Dried and pressed leaves were used as bookmarks, particularly in prayer books. In the time of Queen Elizabeth I, Alecost leaves were scattered on the floor or placed in wardrobes and linen cupboards as an aromatic and a disinfectant.

The dried leaves are separated from the stalks, and may be made into powder which is kept in airtight containers. The powder tends to be stronger than the fresh leaves.

Alecost is used medicinally in a number of ways. Herbalists have praised it for its strengthening effect on the stomach, for its anodyne effect on headaches, and as an agent for healing the liver and spleen. Its healing properties have, however, probably been exaggerated. The crushed fresh leaves soothe abrasions and insect bites. It was once used to flavour beer, before hops were introduced.

It can be grown in a warm, sunny spot in the garden and it is propagated by the division of clumps, preferably about once every three years.

Tansy

Tanacetum vulgare L.,
syn. *Chrysanthemum vulgare* (L.) Beruh.

This is a perennial herb of the family Compositae. It has a robust, erect, grooved, square stem, bearing alternate, palmatisect, bright green leaves. The yellow flowerheads are arranged in dense corymbs. The central flowers are bisexual and the outer ones are female.

Tansy grows in Europe and Asia, and is found wild alongside roads and streams, in shrubberies and fields. It has a strong, camphor-like smell and a spicy, bitter taste. Some people find the strong smell rather disagreeable.

However, Tansy was popular as an aromatic herb and the English once even preferred it to Mint. Its most common use in olden times was in the preserving of fish and meat, as its strong smell disguised that of the stale meat. Tansy is only very rarely used today, usually to flavour cakes and milk puddings.

As a medicinal herb, Tansy contains essential oils with the active principle thujone, the bitter principle tanacetin, resins and waxes. In very small doses, it is beneficial to the human body, stimulating appetite and digestion.

It was also used to cure nausea brought about by gluttony after fasting for Lent. Large doses are poisonous, but it can be applied externally to sprained joints and to ease rheumatism. It was once used as a poison, and for embalming the dead and as a dye for fabrics.

It is often cultivated in gardens, but the old herbalists claimed that the wild variety was more aromatic and more efficacious. The plant was probably first cultivated in monastery gardens from which it escaped to grow wild.

Cacao

Theobroma cacao L.

This is a tropical, evergreen tree, 5 to 8m (15 to 24ft) high with a dense, spherical crown. It belongs to the family Steruliaceae. It is cultivated extensively for its seeds. Cacao first forms clusters of pink flowers on the trunk and larger branches. These are later transformed into longish, smooth, or length-wise grooved pods reminiscent of yellow or orange marrows. The fruits seem to grow straight from the trunk.

Cacao is native to tropical America but is cultivated on a large scale elsewhere, particularly in Africa. The fruits are hidden in a thick protective covering which contains 20 to 40 flat or rounded seeds known as 'cocoa beans'. Each seed is encased in a pinkish, brownish or off-white pulp with a slightly sour taste and smell.

Normally the fruits are stored after harvesting, and then they are skinned, fermented, washed and dried. The beans are roasted and ground into cocoa mixture which is then divided by hot pressing into cocoa butter and cocoa powder. The mixture is most frequently made into edible chocolate.

Both cocoa and chocolate contain the alkaloid theobromine and traces of caffeine. Although less stimulating than caffeine, theobromine has a tonic effect and helps counteract physical and mental fatigue.

In Latin America chocolate is used in a number of different dishes.

Pork Cutlets with Chocolate Sauce

4 pork cutlets
1 × 15ml spoon (1 tablespoon) oil
3 onions, peeled and chopped
salt
black pepper
pinch cinnamon
100g (4oz) field mushrooms, sliced
100ml (4fl oz) white wine

2 cloves garlic, peeled and chopped
50g (2oz) almonds
1 × 15ml spoon (1 tablespoon) parsley
1 × 15ml spoon (1 tablespoon) oil
300ml (1/2pint) consommé
50g (2oz) bitter chocolate or cocoa powder

Season the cutlets with salt and pepper and baste with oil. Grill for 10 minutes on each side. Keep warm. Fry the chopped onion and garlic in oil until just coloured, add the sliced mushrooms and seasoning and cook until the mushrooms are tender. Add the wine and chopped almonds and continue cooking. Melt the chocolate and consommé in a pan, and bring to the boil. Then pour over the cooked vegetable mixture, to which the cutlets have been added, and cook for another 5 minutes.

Serves 4

Wild Thyme

Thymus serpyllum L.

A perennial plant of the family Labiatae, Wild Thyme grows to a height of about 25cm (10in) with reddish, rooting stems. The small, opposite leaves are ovate in shape. The flowers are scarlet, pale pink or white, arranged in capitula. It is a melliferous plant flowering from May to September.

Wild Thyme grows in Europe, America and central and northern Africa. It is found on dry sloping ground and in fields and roadsides in sunny places. It can be used both as a seasoning and medicinally.

The leaves and stalks, gathered early in the flowering period, are used as a seasoning, generally in dried form. The best-flavoured Wild Thyme comes from plants grown in sunny spots. Wild Thyme has a strong, pungent smell and a spicy, slightly bitter taste. Both the young shoots and flowers can be picked and dried in well-ventilated conditions. It should be stored in a tightly closed container away from the light.

Wild Thyme is used as an ingredient of mixed herbs, and as a flavouring for meat and vegetable stews, pulse soups, hamburgers and vegetable pies. It is also used in stuffings for roast meat, game and poultry.

It contains essential oils with cymol and thymol, flavones, phytoncides, a high content of tannins and other constituents. Used medicinally, it relieves coughs and flatulence and has antimycotic effects.

Meat Bake with Wild Thyme

400g (14oz) cooked minced beef
2 × 15ml spoons (2 tablespoons) oil
2 cloves garlic
2 × 15ml spoons (2 tablespoons) parsley
1 × 2.5ml spoon (1/2 teaspoon) wild thyme

8 tomatoes
salt
pepper
2 × 15ml spoons (2 tablespoons) grated cheese (or more, according to taste)
2 × 15ml spoons (2 tablespoons) breadcrumbs

Grease an ovenproof dish with oil, and then add half the sliced tomatoes, chopped parsley, salt and crushed garlic. Cover with a layer of minced meat, sprinkle with more seasoning and garlic, then finish with another layer of tomatoes, seasoning, garlic. Top with grated cheese and breadcrumbs and bake in a hot oven for 20 minutes.

Serves 4

Garden Thyme

Thymus vulgaris L.

A small perennial semi-shrub of the family Labiatae, Garden Thyme grows 15 to 40cm (6 to 16in) high; it is densely branched with stems which are woody in the lower part, and covered with small, opposite, linear and pulescent leaves. The flowers, which are clustered in the axils of the leaves are small, pink, pinkish purple and scarlet. Flowering occurs in May and June. The plant is aromatic and melliferous.

Garden Thyme was originally native to the western parts of the Mediterranean. It has been used for centuries, and had a sacred significance; the Egyptians used it for embalming. It first began to be used as a pot-herb in the Middle Ages and was recommended by the herbalists of those days as a flavouring for sauces and used dry, crushed and mixed with salt, as a condiment for a wide variety of dishes.

The leaves are collected in the flowering period, and may be used dried or fresh. When sold it is usually shredded, although stripped whole leaves and flowers are of better quality. Good-quality Thyme should be grey-green in colour with a pungent scent and strong, slightly acrid taste.

Thyme is used a great deal in all Mediterranean and North African cooking, as well as in central European cooking. It mixes well with other spices and is used for flavouring game, beef, cheese, sauces, salads, pulses, fish, pizza, pâté and stewed vegetables. Mixed with Bay and Juniper it is used to season sauerkraut and pickled vegetables. Mixed with other herbs it makes a seasoning for soup and stews.

It contains an essential oil (up to 2 per cent) with cymol, thymol and carvacrol, and 10 per cent tannins, bitter principles, saponins, flavones and resins.

Medicinally, it has deodorant, disinfectant and anthelmintic properties, curing stomach inflammations, flatulence, diarrhoea and promoting good digestion. Large doses should not be taken in pregnancy or by people with cardiac trouble. Cultivated Thyme is grown by dividing clumps of the existing plants, or by sowing seed in light, lime-rich, sandy soil. Garden Thyme must have a dry, sunny spot and occasional watering. It can be grown in boxes. It is harvested once or twice a year by cutting.

Fenugreek

Trigonella foenum-graecum L.

Fenugreek is an annual plant of the Papilionaceae family which grows up to 50cm (20in) high. It has an erect, slightly branched stem with trimerous leaves with dentate margins. The flowers are pale yellow. The fruit is a narrow, sabre-shaped pod up to 10cm (4in) long with a protracted tip. It contains up to 20 grooved, oblong, green-brown seeds. The whole plant has a spicy smell and resembles lucerne.

It is native to Asia and is found in the wild in the Mediterranean region. It is cultivated in many parts of the world and was known centuries ago in Egypt as a fever-reducing drug.

The seeds are used as a seasoning and are highly aromatic with a bitter aftertaste. They are normally used in powder form.

Fenugreek is used in mixed spices: for example, in Indian curry powder. It is used in Bulgarian cooking in a special recipe which combines it with savory, hot peppers and maize flour. Fenugreek is also used to flavour cheese and, in India, roasted Fenugreek seeds make a substitute for coffee.

Fenugreek contains a high percentage of mucilages (up to 30 per cent) a lot of proteins, fats, saponins, alkaloids (trigonellin), flavones. It also contains a large amount of iron, phosphorus, tannins, cholin and bitter principles. It regulates the activity of the digestive tract and strengthens the organism, improving the metabolism. It reduces the content of sugar in the blood and lowers blood pressure.

Fenugreek has to be grown in sunny places in light, lime-rich soil. The seeds are sown just below the surface of the soil in rows 25cm (10in) apart.

Périgord Truffle

Tuber melanosporum Vittadini

Piedmont Truffle

Tuber magnatum Pico

Common Earth-ball

Scleroderma aurantium Persoon

There are several different types of fungi used for seasoning. One of the most famous is the Périgord Truffle which has been renowned for centuries in France. Its fruit-bodies have a black, warty skin and are found in the soil of oak forests in the south of France. The fruits grow underground and are highly aromatic. They are hunted out by trained dogs or pigs. The truffles are used as a stuffing and for flavouring pâté and salami.

Northern Italy also has its own type of truffle: the Piedmont Truffle. There are several varieties of this type of truffle. One of them, *Choiromyces meandriformis,* is used exclusively as a seasoning. The fruit-bodies are tuberous and vary in size — the biggest can weigh up to 500g (1lb). The fruit-bodies, which are grey-white when young turning to reddish-brown when mature, are also aromatic.

The Common Earth-ball *(Scleroderma aurantium)* has spherical or uneven-shaped bodies which protrude just above the soil. Only the young white fruit-bodies are collected. It is so aromatic that only a few slices should be used and larger amounts are dangerous.

Top: *Tuber melanosporum*
Centre: *Tuber magnatum*
Bottom: *Scleroderma aurantium*

Stinging Nettle

Urtica dioica L.

This perennial plant of the family Urticaceae can reach a height of 1m (3ft). The creeping rootstalk sends out square stems bearing pointed opposite leaves with serrate margins. It is dioecious (the male and female flowers grow separately). The whole plant is covered by stinging hairs. Besides the Stinging Nettle, the shorter Small Nettle *(Urtica urens)* can be used in cooking.

The nettle is a common weed distributed throughout Europe. It will grow almost anywhere where the soil is rich in nitrogen.

For cooking, only the young tops are used. These are collected in early spring (the old leaves are too tough), washed thoroughly, and cooked in boiling, salted water, like spinach. The taste is not dissimilar to spinach, in fact, and the stinging element of the nettle is destroyed in cooking.

Nettles contain a number of vitamins — C, carotene, K, E, E_2, and the pantotene acid. Nettles also contain a series of organic acids (silicic and formic), acetylcholin, histamine, a high percentage of chlorophyll, anti-bacterial substances (phytoncides), many mineral components (iron, magnesium, calcium, silicon, manganese), lecithine, tannins, secretin, mucilages and waxes. Nettles are a good antidote to spring fatigue. They strengthen the organism and reduce the blood sugar level. They affect the formation of red corpuscles and promote the activity of the kidney, liver and gall bladder, as well as regulating the peristalsis.

Nettles can be added to soups, mixed with spinach, or blended into omelettes. They can be mixed with dandelion salad and served as a vegetable accompanying meat, flavoured with a little garlic, onion and nutmeg, butter, pepper and salt.

Wild Herb and Potato Salad

500g (1lb) potatoes, boiled
2 × 15ml spoons (2 tablespoons) mixed
   herbs: nettle, sorrel, cress, dand-
   elion, ground ivy, ribwort, parsley

1 small onion, finely chopped
vinaigrette dressing

Cut the potatoes into small cubes and mix with the remaining ingredients. Toss in vinaigrette dressing. Chill before serving. Mayonnaise can be used instead of the vinaigrette dressing if preferred.

European Corn Salad
(also known as **Lamb's Lettuce**)
Valerianella locusta (L.) Betcke

This is an annual plant of the family Valerianaceae which grows up to 10 to 30cm (4 to 12in) high. The upper oblong leaves are used as a seasoning and vegetable. The plant produces capitula of small bluish to white flowers.

European Corn Salad is a wild plant which is found on grassy land and embankments. Improved varieties are cultivated, especially in Germany and northern Europe.

Only the fresh young leaves are used as a seasoning and vegetable. They can be made into salad or stewed like spinach. They can also be used to flavour cheese spreads, soups and lettuce.

The plant is rich in vitamin C. It also contains carotene, vitamins B_1, B_2, phosphorus, calcium and iron. Sugars, proteins, fats and other substances are also present. It is a good antidote to spring fatigue and helps to improve digestion.

Corn Salad can be grown on almost any soil. It is sown in summer to be harvested the same autumn, or in autumn to be harvested the following spring. The whole leafy rosette can be used.

Lettuce with Corn Salad

2 heads of lettuce
2 corn salad rosettes
30g (1oz) melted butter
2 cloves garlic

1 × 15ml spoon (1 tablespoon) lemon
    juice
pinch sugar, salt

Wash and drain the lettuce and corn salad, and tear into small pieces. Mix the melted butter, crushed garlic, lemon juice, sugar and salt and pour over the salad before serving.

Vanilla

Vanilla planifolia Andrews

Vanilla is a perennial tropical climbing herb of the family Orchidaceae. It has a long, pulpous, hairless, cylindrical stem. Flat fleshy leaves grow from nodes on the stem, as do white aerial roots which later replace the original root system. The flowers are arranged in axil clusters. There is only one stamen without loose pollen. In Mexico, where vanilla originated, pollination is carried out by Melipona bees. Elsewhere pollination is artificial. After pollination, a thin long capsule is formed from the ovary. It is semi-pulpous and filled with a black, mushy substance which contains a large number of tiny, non-germinative seeds. The capsules, after processing, provide the seasoning.

Vanilla is indigenous to tropical America, in particular to Mexico, where it still grows wild. It is cultivated elsewhere in the tropics, and the cultivated variety is more aromatic than the wild one. The full flavour of Vanilla is only achieved if the processing, fermentation and drying are correct.

Vanilla, crushed or ground, may be used as a seasoning for pastries and drinks, and is used principally in the manufacture of chocolate, sweets and liqueurs.

The aroma of Vanilla is caused by a substance known as vanillin, which is formed in processing. Good-quality Vanilla has about 2.5 to 4.5 per cent of vanillin. A small quantity of heliotropin is also present. The Aztecs and Toltecs used Vanilla medicinally. They believed it strengthened the heart, eliminated tiredness and protected against fever.

Ginger

Zingiber officinale Rosc.

Ginger is a perennial plant of the family Zingiberaceae. It is a monocotyledon. It has reed-like leaves and is cultivated for its pulpy, tuber-like, thickened rhizomes which grow up to 10cm (4in) long, are knotted and flattened on both sides. Ginger does not seed itself, but is propagated exclusively in the vegetative manner.

It is cultivated in the tropics, particularly in India, China, Japan, Jamaica and West Africa. It has a long history and was mentioned in old Chinese manuscripts. It was also known to the Romans and Greeks and was not discovered in Europe until the Middle Ages.

Dried or ground Ginger is added to various spice mixtures, curry being one of the best known. It is used as a flavouring in breads and cakes and to flavour meat, poultry and fish. Ginger is used fresh in Asian cooking and it is also preserved, sliced, in salt or sugar. It is an important agent in liqueur manufacture. It is also used to flavour drinks — ginger beer and ale, for example.

Ginger contains some 2 per cent volatile oil, ginger essential oil, and a sharp, pungent substance called gingerol. The rhizomes are processed into oil and essences and are dried and ground to make the seasoning.

Ginger does well in light, humus-rich soil. It is grown in the shade of other crops because it is sensitive to strong sunlight. When the stems dry off, the rootstalks are ploughed out, dried and processed.

Index of English Names

Index of Latin Names